KU-225-261

James Hunt
Against
All Odds

Eoin Young with James Hunt
Edited by David Hodges

Hamlyn
London·New York·Sydney·Toronto

Acknowledgements

The publishers are grateful to the following
individuals and organizations for the illustrations in
this book: *Autocar*; *Autosport*; Cor Bruninsma;
Diana Burnett; Jack Curtis, *Reveille*; D.P.P.I.; *Daily
Express*; Dutch Motor Racing Photos; Jutta Fausel;
A. Foster, *Daily Mirror*; Geoffrey Goddard; David
Hodges; Keystone Press Agency; Foto-Kräling;
London Art Tech; Mike Marchant; Marlboro;
Douglas Morrison; *Motor*; Arthur Partridge; Phipps
Photographic; Press Association; Maurice Rowe;
Nigel Snowdon; John Starr, All Sport; Gerry Stream;
Syndication International; Peter Tempest; Texaco;
David Winter

Published by The Hamlyn Publishing Group Limited
London · New York · Sydney · Toronto
Astronaut House, Feltham, Middlesex, England
Copyright © Overseas Motor Racing Enterprises Ltd.

ISBN 0 600 35250 1

Filmset in Great Britain by Tradespools Limited, Frome, Somerset
Printed in Great Britain by Hazell, Watson & Viney Limited,
Aylesbury, Buckinghamshire

Contents

Introduction

Had 1976 not been the most dramatic season ever in the history of motor racing this book would never have been written.

For some time now, in fact ever since I was first approached on the subject, I vowed that I would not 'do a book' until after I retired from driving. I naturally want the book to be as interesting as possible and to that end I believe that most people would like to read about what went on inside *the Grand Prix world and* inside *my head during my complete career. Such a book written now would be both incomplete and the probable end of my career! Besides I have seen too many people in similar positions being pressured by commercial interests into producing hurried diaries of their day to day activities which have already been chronicled by the media.*

However circumstances have forced me to compromise because my refusal to embark on an autobiography has already prompted one publisher to produce a biography of me which was less than accurate.

I made this exception to my rule because 1976 was an exceptional year. Despite the mass of words that have already been published on the subject we have not seen a concise, interesting and cohesive story of the season as a whole; this book is an attempt to achieve that.

Eoin Young is probably the best writer in the motor racing business and although he has written the story largely from my point of view and with my collaboration I feel that we have achieved our object and produced an accurate and interesting story of the 1976 season. It is difficult to be objective when reading about oneself so I can only hope that you agree with me.

JH
Marbella
March 1977

Prologue

James Simon Wallis Hunt was born in a nursing home in Sutton, Surrey, on August 29, 1947, son of stockbroker Wallis Hunt, who, if he thought about motor racing at all in those difficult post-war days, would have regarded it as a pastime for people with a degree more money than sense. James was a brother for Sally, aged two, and there were to be three more brothers – Peter, Timothy and David – before a second sister, Georgina, arrived in the Hunt household.

James went to Ambleside school in Cheam and then to Northlace in Sutton before being sent to Westerleigh boarding preparatory school in Sussex at the age of eight. When he was 13 he moved on to his father's old school, Wellington College in Berkshire, where all four Hunt boys received their education. Academic work had to compete with sport for James, and while his scholastic record was acceptable, he was making a name for himself in tennis, racquets and cross-country running. He played Junior Wimbledon tennis, squash for Surrey, and still runs five or six miles a day to keep in shape for his racing. His father was keen that James should follow a profession, and he was already entered for medical school when on his 18th birthday in 1965 he went with friends to a race meeting at Silverstone. It sparked an instant ambition. Suddenly he knew he wanted to be world champion racing driver. Eleven years after watching a motor race for the first time, James Hunt was on his way to achieving that ambition. He celebrated his 29th birthday in the paddock at Zandvoort after winning the Dutch Grand Prix for the second time.

Today Hunt is an almost hippy figure with a forthright disregard for convention, lounging in tee shirt and jeans, living in the south of Spain, a socialite, comfortable in a discotheque or at a party. He seems poles apart in personality from his 1976 championship rival Niki Lauda, who conveys the chill calm of an engineer, a driver dedicated to the development of his car, who eats, drinks and sleeps motor racing. Neither man had much more than raw talent and fierce ambition when they first stepped into Grand Prix cars, reaching towards the pinnacle of a driver's career in international motor racing.

The structure of motor racing has been likened to a pyramid, with the world championship as its pinnacle supported by ever-broader layers. Most drivers, and Hunt was no exception, serve an apprenticeship and progress through these layers towards the pin-nacle – or in most cases, part of the way towards it. The *ab initio* low-priced single-seater class where Hunt started to learn his craft was Formula Ford, for cars using 1·6 litre Ford production engines (Formula Ford is popular in many countries, and there are also equivalent 'first step' classes such as Formula Vee using Volkswagen engines, Formule Renault, and Formula Italia using Fiat power units).

Formula 3 is an international class for cars with 2-litre production-based engines fitted with a device to limit power output, while Formula 2 is for single seaters with 2-litre racing engines. From time to time the regulations governing these international formulae are changed, so that, for example, when James Hunt started racing in Formula 3 the engine capacity limit was 1 litre.

Very often the top drivers 'grow up' together through these steps to the Grands Prix, and quite early in his career Hunt raced against some of the men who were to be his rivals for the world championship . . .

Grand Prix in motor racing means, quite simply, Grand Prize, and the grandest prize of all is the Formula 1 World Championship, a title created in 1950 to decide the most successful driver of the year, on a points basis over a number of races. Points are scored in each championship round: nine for a win, six for second, four for third, three for fourth, two for fifth and one for sixth.

Starting positions for each Grand Prix are determined by fastest practice times over two days and three timed sessions. The driver setting the fastest time takes pole position, and can choose to start from the left or right of the front row of the two-by-two grid, depending on which he considers the most favoured side of the track for the run up to the vital first corner.

The world championship adds an extra element of competition to the Grand Prix world, but some argue that the pursuit of championship points can spoil the battle for individual victories, that it can take away something of a race winner's triumph if the race is overshadowed by the championship. Mario Andretti's victory in the 1976 Japanese Grand Prix was an example – with the tense championship situation overwhelming the meeting, how many would remember who had actually won the Grand Prix?

For the 1976 championship was not decided until the eleventh hour, the second to last lap of the 16th and final Grand Prix of the season, and the new champion was James Hunt. He had started the season as the fastest driver in practice for the opening race in Brazil, in his debut for the Marlboro-McLaren team, but setbacks early in the year had made him an unlikely outsider in the championship struggle. By mid-season no gambler would have offered odds on Hunt taking the world championship from the Austrian Niki Lauda, who had won it for Ferrari in 1975. Hunt's fight back brought motor racing to the front pages of newspapers. The world knew that the championship was between Hunt and Lauda when they flew to Tokyo for the race at the foot of Mount Fuji. Even then, few expected that the victor in 1976 would be James Hunt, against all odds.

The Man

James Hunt's heady, early days in Grand Prix racing made him a personality within his sport, and something of a prisoner of his own reputation. He is expected to be flamboyant, colourful and dashing at times when he may prefer to be quiet and relaxed, especially in those vital count-down hours on the morning of a race. In fact, he prefers the company of old friends rather than the 'friends' that fame seems to force upon a successful sportsman. He has time for the specialist press and for the rest of the mediamen who have done their homework, but his patience tends to be on the short side. It is interesting that while the British motoring press would trumpet his championship title, Peter Windsor, the serious young sports editor of *Autocar*, felt that he had not been as close to Hunt as he had been to other drivers in 1976 and 'at a time when public opinion was telling us that Niki Lauda was difficult to get on with, difficult to "promote", I was finding James Hunt well-nigh impossible to talk to'.

Commenting that Hunt destroys the textbook ideal of an ordinary racing driver because he smokes, drinks, has been known to have sex the night before a race, and is also an all-round sportsman to a standard not attained by former world champions or even by others on the current Grand Prix grid, Windsor wrote 'it began to strike me that Hunt's approach to motor racing is very different from the mainstream. As a gifted sportsman first of all, and, secondly, as someone who doesn't have to work hard at being a racing driver, he has above-average belief in himself. This is a difficult thing to describe because all racing drivers appear to be egoists. But with Hunt it is more so.' Hunt's ability to see his performance as independently good or otherwise apart from the car he depends on, his almost disassociated self-confidence, sits easily on his casually clad shoulders.

Grand Prix racing is an exile occupation. There are about 20 top drivers, five of whom are the best in the world and five of whom have the potential to be the best. The other ten are either there for the glamour or the money, on the way up or the way down. All are committed to a gypsy existence for a year, away from home and family. In the 1950s it used to be a dashing thing to do during the European summer, now it's a harrowing endeavour that takes the drivers to a distant confrontation every second weekend. A lot of the glamour has been worn away now – there isn't a lot of glamour about finishing tenth in a Grand Prix any more – and the winners are hard-nosed professionals. Winning and success are what it's all about. Second is losing.

Competing in the
1976 Superstars
series

It was success and the money it brings that exiled James Hunt from England, to escape the British taxation system that can turn success into financial failure. It was the travelling, the Bedouin way of life, always on the move, that parted Hunt and his wife, Susy. Now Hunt bases himself – you can't really consider him as living anywhere, although he does regard it as 'home' – in a rented house beyond Marbella, tucked back towards the hills and away from the beaches. A variety of racing trophies look out of place in the Spanish decor of the house with its cushion-flanked, sunken parlour snug around the open fire. A multilingual, stylish blonde housekeeper looks after him, vets his phone calls and feeds the growing Alsatian named Oscar.

The house has five bedrooms, a patio pool, and garaging for his three-year-old Carrera Porsche, which still proclaims that it is a legacy from his days with the Hesketh racing team. He revels in the car, extols its practicality, the way it swallows the giant young Alsatian, but worries that age and hard use is taking its toll of the clutch, that the fuel lines are starting to perish and the throttle is jamming. He says this is dropping his fuel mileage to 12 to the gallon, adds that on a good day it can be made to return 25, but qualifies this by saying it's awful to drive that way. He is a safe road driver, stays around 70 mph on the open road in Spain and always wears a seat belt, not needing to show every other road user that he is a Grand Prix driver.

The telephone punctuates any conversation, and so does Oscar's adolescent restlessness. For the dog, life is still an adventure with new smells, chickens to chase, other dogs and a small cat flushed

James and Susy

from the long grass to mutual astonishment. *Oscar, OSCAR! No! There's a good boy . . . musn't chase pussies or any little animals. I'm the only one allowed to do that.*

James Hunt, Susy, Richard Burton in December 1976

Oscar has been cautioned against assaults on a scrawny-looking rooster for fear he would get the taste of blood and wipe out the neighbouring poultry population. Hunt is anxious to build up a man–dog relationship with the dog, treating it as a son, schooling it in the difficult ways of the world, gratified when it learns that it can stand up to playful attacks by other local dogs, apprehensively pleased when it is granted probationary associate membership of the golf club.

Because Hunt makes his own rules for living, the breakup of his marriage has not been as traumatic as might have been supposed, beyond the normal human responses to such a situation. He had married Susy, a successful London model, two years earlier. Marriage to James meant settling down, and bringing a stabilizing influence into his life. But it didn't work out that way.

Hunt talks about women and racing, and as he does so he places his long finger on the reason his marriage not so much broke up, as expired.

I prefer to be on my own at races because really there's enough to do looking after me. It's more than I can handle to keep myself under control at a race meeting without trying to look after someone else as well and have more responsibilities and worries. I find that if I want an early night before a race or if I want a couple of hours to cool off and relax before dinner, I can do better to read a book or listen to music, and therefore it's better to be on my own.

Hunt returns to
London Airport as
world champion, to
be greeted by Jane
Birbeck. The
mechanical monkey
is a souvenir of
Japan

He feels this was a major contributing factor, the reason his marriage went wrong.

It was really THE problem. I thought that marriage was what I wanted and needed to give me a nice stable and quiet home life, but in fact it wasn't and the mistake was mine. I really wanted to go racing on my own, and it wasn't much fun for Susy to sit at home and wait for me all that time. It was also a terrible hassle for her to come racing because race meetings were probably the most relaxing time in my schedule. The rest of the time you tend to be leaping on aeroplanes once a day and that made it even worse because it's bad enough organizing one person to get on an aeroplane. Organizing two gets to be twice as much hassle. It got to the point where it was a problem for Susy to come travelling and a hell of a deal for her to stay at home. It was making life miserable in the extreme for her and since I felt responsible for her it was making me miserable too. So we had agreed to split up and then Richard Burton came along and solved all the problems. We had had an immensely successful marriage because I learnt an awful lot about myself and life and I think Susy did too. We all ended up happy, anyway, which is more than can be said for a lot of marriages . . .

That may not be the conventional way of regarding the end of a marriage, but it underlines the fact that James Hunt is not a conventional young man, rather is someone who makes the rules as he goes along.

That doesn't make him a seeker after the trappings of fame and the friendship of the famous, even though he does hasten away from a tape session to play a round of golf with Sean Connery, himself another tax exile to the 'penury' of the Costa del Sol with its backgammon and beaches and winter sunshine. In fact Hunt places a lot of importance on the company of old friends, which itself is unusual since public heroes seem to leave or be left by childhood friends through geography or by a change in the pace or level of life and living. Perhaps the fact that Hunt comes from a large family has something to do with his reliance on, or willingness to be with old friends. Chris Jones, who grew up among the Hunt clan in Cheam, flew out to Japan to see if his friend would win the championship. After James won the British Grand Prix at Brands Hatch he stayed till near midnight drinking with his mates around a barbecue beside their tents in the car park. That is not normal for a Grand Prix winner in an era where a helicopter is almost expected to alight on the finish line and whisk him away. After he had won the title at the end of the season and finally returned home to Marbella, he invited his gang down for the weekend: John 'The Kid' Richardson and his wife Mary, Chris and Susy Jones, and Malcolm and Franny Wood.

Jane Birbeck, the current young lady in James' life, arrived too. They had met a year before when Jane went down to the backgammon competition at Marbella on the arm of Mark McCormack, the American dean of business managers among sports stars whose company handled Hunt until Hunt's brother Peter moved in and took over. They met again in London from time to time, and some months later the relationship blossomed.

Hunt discusses his sex requirements quite frankly, treating it as therapeutic, a relaxation, a form of communication.

I don't usually have sex before a race because I am very definitely concentrating – I find that it is the communication between two people that makes it worthwhile, and before a race I am pretty uncommunicative. However, if say I have an hour or so to spare before dinner on the night before a race then I can enjoy the physical release. But I will only do it with someone who is fully understanding.

If Hunt's treatise on women makes him out to be insufferably chauvinistic and selfish he can turn easily to discussion of the books and music he likes.

I read anything that's light and entertaining but I like variety as well. I like thrillers – obviously they're the easiest and most available things – but I like serious books as well. I quite like educational books although I'm usually frightened to start them. I like to try and learn through reading but I must say I'm not as good at it as I should be. I read a lot and then I stop. I was reading a book in Tokyo and was really into it, then after leaving Japan (following the final Grand Prix of the season) I didn't pick it up again for about a month. It was by Taylor Caldwell . . . a romance . . . very good for me . . .

I love music and it's very important to me in my life. I always take a cassette player when I travel to races and it gives me comfort and relaxation . . . you spend a lot of time on your own, lurking in hotel rooms in strange places and it's nice to have music with you. I like pop and I like classical music. I like Beethoven particularly. The trumpet? It's the only instrument I can play but unfortunately it's hopeless to play for pleasure on your own. You have to be very good to make a nice noise completely solo on the trumpet . . . and I'm just not good enough.

Travel is another major part of a Grand Prix driver's life and Hunt has his own way of handling the thousands of miles covered annually getting to and from the race circuits.

I always make a point of relaxing when I travel. That's the golden rule. No matter what the difficulties and the problems are – and there are always a lot of very annoying things about tickets and standing in queues – it's always a positive disadvantage to get uptight. It gets you backwards rather than forwards and so you just take all the annoyance as it comes and relax, otherwise you waste yourself while you're travelling. You have to look at the plane seat as a comfortable armchair with a good book and no telephone. Flying doesn't bother me. I don't mind the long distances. The tiring part about flying is going through the airports . . . especially when there are a lot of changes. I find that I can take catnaps easily on a plane journey and I can wake refreshed.

Ironically for someone so relaxed, Hunt is famous for his short fuse, what passes for temper or temperament, but which he describes as a calculated letting off steam.

There's really a very simple explanation. You run for four days and you keep your emotions under lock and key. When the race stops or if I've retired from the race, as soon as I get out of the car the pent-up emotions are ready to leap out. In the car they're kept under control. I think it's a normal and human way to behave, and if it upsets anyone that's unfortunate.

Winning doesn't damp the fuse after it has smouldered for the weekend. Hunt recalls an incident after he had won the 1976 Spanish Grand Prix at Jarama. It had been a tiring race and from somewhere he had secured a bottle of orange juice in the crush of getting out of his car and going to the royal box for the presentation.

I'd just won the race, I was tired and thirsty and this drink was the only thing I had in the world. This guy knocked it out of my hand and I punched him. It was a terrible thing to do because the poor guy hadn't meant to but I didn't have time to think about it. I felt awful about it afterwards and tried to find him to apologize, but I couldn't find him. I'm not a punchy person normally, but I'm always punchy when I get out of the car.

When he is driving, Hunt says he keeps very cold and stays in control, but he tells a story of 'Bubbles' Horsley, the Hesketh team manager, playing tricks on him in the pits in practice, holding out slow signals, telling the mechanics to work slowly, knowing it would infuriate Hunt who can't tolerate indolence, simply to spark him on to greater efforts through being aroused.

Teddy Mayer says Hunt tends to get angry momentarily but that the anger passes quickly. 'I suppose it's not a bad way for a driver to be. They've got to have some fire and determination and at least if he blows off steam, it's gone. If he carried it around bottled up it could do all sorts of harm. So I don't see that as a particularly bad characteristic. It might be unpleasant for a few moments but you can learn to live with that.'

Hunt is his own coach and trainer when it comes to discipline before a race. As a social animal he enjoys parties but the partying stops the weekend before a race.

The daily jog

A classic cover
drive . . .

I don't drink from the Tuesday before a race because I do weight training and Tuesday is traditionally my last hard training day. I have light training exercises on Wednesday, and on Thursday I have nothing because generally in Europe that's the day I'm travelling to the race. From Wednesday night any form of alcohol is absolutely taboo for me. It's purely personal discipline because there is no harm at all in having a glass of wine with dinner or even two glasses of wine. Or a beer. It's just a matter of principle and if you make a rule for yourself, you've got to stick to it. I know plenty of drivers who have a glass of wine with their dinner. Nothing wrong with that at all; it can't possibly do any harm by any stretch of the imagination, but I have my rule that I don't. I mean who wants one glass of wine anyway? If I'm going to have some wine, I want ten glasses. . .

As a youth, Hunt was quite a sportsman, playing squash to county standards and making a name for himself at Wellington College as a cross-country runner. As yet there are no squash courts in Marbella but courts are being built. Every day he runs from his house down to the main Malaga/Cadiz road, a return jog of just over $2\frac{1}{2}$ miles. He plays golf a lot and some tennis. He blames his physical exercises, or the vigour of them, for setting up or at least aggravating the inflamed nerve in his left elbow which put him in enough pain to call for pain-killing injections before the 1976 US Grand Prix.

Tennis is a very difficult game. As a boy I played tennis quite well but the trouble is, to play tennis well you've got to practise and play a lot. I don't really have the time or the inclination to do that and I find it frustrating to play a game badly even when I'm not used to playing it.

He reflects that he would not have reached the same heights in any of the other sports in which he has shown more than promise. *Probably my best game was squash, and I might have reached a very high group in the world – I might have got into the top ten if I'd worked at it with total dedication, but not the top five, as I didn't have the talent to be tops.*

As a world champion, his earning power is obviously enormous, although probably not disproportionate when compared with other sports, where the stars can in any case expect to have longer active playing careers at the top.

There comes a stage in the career of every top racing driver when

Right: Hunt
relaxing
competitively and
(**following pages**)
at home with Oscar

winning races seems to be the easiest part. The marketing properties
of a Grand Prix driver are a phenomenon of the 1970s, sparked by
the hustling ambition of Jackie Stewart who out-drove and out-sold
his rivals to establish himself as the first executive-style Grand Prix
driver. Before Stewart it had been a sport with vague ideas about
being a business; successful and wealthy drivers had banked their
winnings, but they weren't selling themselves away from the race
track. John Young Stewart was anxious to establish himself as a
brand name in his own right, and to forge the connotations of
quality he aimed high. He linked his name with Rolex watches,
Moët & Chandon champagne, Glenfiddich malt whisky, and
British Airways. When he retired he stayed close to his racing sponsors and retained consultancy contracts with Goodyear, Ford and
the French Elf oil company.

Much of Stewart's business management is handled through the
international offices of golfing promoter Mark McCormack, and
when James Hunt looked like being the next superstar to emerge
from the Grand Prix grid, he became one of McCormack's clients.
But it was an uneasy alliance. Where Stewart had been able to set
up and sort out many of his own business deals with background
assistance from the McCormack men, Hunt had to rely more
heavily on his business managers and he felt it wasn't working out.

Hunt with his
brother and
manager Peter
('Norman') at the
Austrian GP in 1976

Peter Hunt, James' younger brother, describes the situation.
'When James signed with McCormack's organization in September
1973, the London firm in which I'm a partner was already advising

James on tax matters. It was arranged that we would continue to advise on special tax matters and that McCormack's organization would handle the business side.'

In March 1974 it became obvious that the price for Hunt's growing success would have to be paid, and the decision was taken for him to become a tax exile, to comply with regulations and live outside Britain. On balance, Peter Hunt feels that the British public has come to accept the fact that successful personalities who earn a lot of money often have a relatively short span of peak earning capacity and they have to go abroad or exert their considerable talents on behalf of the British tax man. 'It would be different if James was the only sportsman or personality to have left the country for that reason, but it has become pretty much the accepted thing these days.'

While he was at Monaco in 1974, James telephoned his brother and asked him if he would consider leaving his desk in the City to come and work for him. The brothers eventually decided on a compromise whereby Peter stayed with his firm in London and handled James' affairs from there. Peter went to the Dutch Grand Prix a month later and worked out an arrangement with the McCormack men to operate jointly until their contract expired at the end of the year and the situation would be reviewed. As it worked out, Peter Hunt took over responsibility for his brother's affairs. His office took over James's accounts, bookwork, diary and fan mail and the McCormack contract terminated on an amicable basis.

For James it meant that he was able to be freed from the high-pressure American business approach and to operate more easily with his brother.

I'm fortunate to be able to work with Pete who is a chartered accountant and now runs a little department within his firm which looks after people like me and one or two other drivers and sportsmen. He does everything as far as my management is concerned. I suppose I see perhaps a tenth of the total business operation that goes through the office in Welbeck Street; Pete deals with it entirely and only the important things are discussed with me for decisions. He administrates the whole deal and wet-nurses me as well. When I want more socks I phone up from wherever I happen to be in the world and they send someone out to Marks and Spencer's to buy me more socks. So that side of it is great. It means I can concentrate entirely on getting on with my job, and when I'm not working I can relax entirely. I don't have to keep rushing into an office and checking on who has paid and who hasn't, and keep track of my mail. It's all done for me.

My main sponsorship contracts are Marlboro, Texaco, Vauxhall and Goodyear. I enjoy a very good relationship with them and Pete is one of the most important reasons for that, because the big company people respect how efficiently my affairs are run. It makes it easy for them to deal with me, and I believe that has helped me enormously. I honestly believe that if one of the traditional sports management organizations had been handling my affairs and been rushing in with the hard sell, I wouldn't have the two-years contract with Texaco that I have now. I'm sure it's because they respect the way our business is carried out.

I hate being involved with promotions if the guy who hired you hasn't done a good job of setting it up, because it reflects badly on you. It doesn't satisfy me, just to get my cheque at the end of the day. That's the nice thing about my sponsors – they give me sensible work to do. I can see the value in it for them and it means one goes away at the end of the day, satisfied that one has been of worthwhile value for money. It's most important.

According to team manager Mayer, the major portion of Hunt's racing contract fee is paid by Marlboro and Texaco. 'Our part of the driver's fee comes in terms of prize money, so our percentage depends on that and obviously this year James did very well. We pay him 40 per cent of the prize money his car earns which is a fairly standard arrangement in most teams. This year he didn't have a bonus arrangement if he won the world championship but for 1977 he will have.' Top drivers can earn in excess of £500,000 annually.

Bike race in Brazil 1977. Hunt v Lauda again?

I do my deals with the team and my sponsors and to an extent that's the end of the story. I get my percentages as I race, and the better I do in races the better I do financially. But the races are still a sporting effort for my own personal achievement, and I really don't think about the money too much. Obviously one attempts to capitalize, but to find a happy medium. One wants to win races, one wants to live a nice life, one wants to make as much money as one reasonably can without becoming a sort of machine.

Even at the peak of his racing career, world champion James Hunt has some firm ideas about retirement.

It is my ambition to retire, but I want to do it from the top, not from the dreaded slide down. It's not any immediate thing for me although I've now got the championship behind me. I've signed with McLaren and Marlboro for

1977 and 1978, and I'm sure I will race for another year after that. I've given no thought to what I would do when I retire, but there are obviously a few more years carrying on with all the business you get into with racing sponsors and associated companies, even though you've stopped driving. A couple of years at least before people forget you and your earning potential goes down. I shall want to see through what I've built up, without trying to build it up any further, and as that winds down I'll wind myself into something else.

I can't see myself having any rest from now until I retire, so the first thing I'll deserve is a holiday – I won't physically go on holiday, but I'll try and wind down the pace of my life a bit, take it a bit easier but still go to the races and do the things that one gets involved with. I have no plans as to what I might do or where I would live, because I'm quite busy enough doing what I'm doing at the moment to wonder about what I'm going to do then.

In common with most other leading drivers of recent years, Hunt parts company with died-in-the-wool enthusiasts when racing traditions and the past are concerned – they just do not enter into his scheme of things.

Probably when I retire I will look back to the traditional things, and then perhaps I will reflect that it was a pity that – say – the International Trophy at Silverstone lost some of its status in 1977. But while I am racing that sort of thing is not high on my list because it is not relevant. I can't even live in the past with myself, my mind works in the present and has to keep moving on with something approaching total concentration. Naturally I do not concentrate 24 hours a day on how I am going to drive the next race, but I do have to build up to the future – there isn't room, there isn't time or space, to look back, and I have to live with the times as far as races are concerned.

He has very little time for the Establishment of racing (none at all for the 'counts and princes without qualifications' among the hierarchy), and he would like to see the sport controlled by professionals – that is something he feels must come. Individual race organizers range from good to bad, while some of the entrepreneurs of the sport obviously rate highly in his book – he quotes John Webb of Brands Hatch as an example.

Throughout, Hunt comes through as a modern professional sportsman, as vital in his own special field as a surging current outside the slow mainstream of routine jobs. On the subject of his ability to drive a racing car, Teddy Mayer says 'I would say of all the drivers we've had, James has the greatest natural talent – by far, in fact. Possibly he makes more mistakes than, say, Emerson* but he certainly is quicker than Emerson ever was when he drove for us and I think James is as consistently fast a driver as anyone I've ever seen. I would begin to compare his talent in the last half of the 1976 season with Jackie Stewart's in his ability to win races driving a car that, in my opinion, is about the same as many others. Drivers like Jimmy Clark generally won races because they had superior cars. I think James' car is good, but I don't think it's any better than several other cars. Possibly it's more reliable, but it's quick because he's quick. . . .'

---

* Who to some observers drives as though he's on rails.

Early Days in Racing

One of James Hunt's first important career decisions was not to go to medical school, much to the distress of his parents. Instead he attacked a variety of jobs to finance his new-found passion for motor racing. He was an icecream salesman, a porter in an hospital, a can stacker in a supermarket and a hospital van driver. He even wanted to be a bus conductor, but was turned down because he was too tall.

In this way he scraped together enough money to buy a stripped Mini shell, which was to take him almost two years to build into a raceworthy car. Ironically, in view of the scrutineering dramas that were to come in 1976, Hunt's Mini was turned away from the scrutineering bay at the Snetterton circuit at its first race meeting because it had neither windscreen nor side windows.

The Mini was Hunt's racing kindergarten and he was soon looking beyond it. The logical progression for an aspiring world champion was to move from a Mini into an open-wheel single seater to gain experience, and he took the now-traditional step into Formula Ford, with an Alexis. This was bought on hire purchase, £300 down

A youthful James Hunt in his Formula Ford days

Top: up a rung of
the racing ladder
and into Formula 3,
lining up his
Brabham BT21 for
Paddock Bend at
Brands Hatch and
followed by Hanson
and Bond

Above: Hunt's
Lotus 59 running
wide as he leads a
bunch of cars onto
the Brands Hatch
long circuit in 1970

and £100 his father had planned to give him on his 21st birthday,
brought forward a few months. When a budding racing driver
moves into any form of single seater it tends to mean that his racing
is becoming more than a hobby. How serious he is depends on his
skill and his will to win.

Hunt raced that Alexis for the first time at Snetterton and finished
in his own words 'about fifth', a little despondent at his car's lack
of performance compared with others using the same Ford engine.
Then he found the cause of that problem – his ignition distributor
had been incorrectly set. With an extra 15 bhp at his command in
his next race he finished second to the acknowledged pace-maker
Tony Trimmer, and a week later won a race at Lydden Hill in Kent.

In 1969 he graduated to Formula 3, although the term 'graduate'
tends to be relative in racing.

*Formula 3 was the right way to go, particularly at that time – it was the only
place for an up-and-coming driver, the only serious route into Formula 1. So
I naturally followed it, and I started with a two-year-old Brabham BT21
and an engine that was three years old. But the BT21 was a hell of a good*

car, and that one was well prepared. We only raced in England, doing half a dozen or so races towards the end of 1969. I had a very good time, and managed to do very well in what was an old car. In fact, it was probably more competitive than people thought. It obviously impressed some of the right people, for it got me a Grovewood Award.

Hunt was in a class of racing where even last month's car may be out of date, but he made up for the Brabham's age with his cockpit ability. At Cadwell Park he shared the lap record, and was actually leading Ronnie Peterson on the last lap of the race when, by his own admission, he made a mistake and paid for it by finishing a modest fourth after a stirring race. Peterson had been driving the first March, and Hunt's efforts in the old Brabham were obviously impressive because when Peterson was injured in a crash at Montlhéry, Hunt was offered the works drive. A works drive, even as a substitute driver, might be regarded as a definite step up in any driver's career, and Hunt normally recalls his 'milestone' cars with some affection. But he dismisses that March very tersely: *That isn't one of the cars I would ask to have another go in!*

His success at the end of 1969 meant that he was able to arrange some sponsorship to run a Lotus 59 in 1970, and he contested Continental races as a member of a happy band who lived a gypsy existence, trailing their racing cars from event to event in what is now recalled as a halcyon period of Formula 3.

We didn't really have enough sponsorship, but I managed to struggle through to the Pau meeting at the beginning of May, where I ran out of money completely. We managed to scrape together enough to get to the next race, and then started living off income – we actually ran the team off income for the rest of the year, which was quite an achievement in 1970, just by plodding round, living in a tent and collecting start money. It was always a struggle, and it meant that I didn't really have the best equipment or enough spares.

It was good for me, because it taught me a lot of things about driving, and it certainly taught me to keep out of trouble. 'Hunt the Shunt' hadn't come into existence then, and in fact I had hardly any accident damage that year. My accident bill was about £600, and the one well-publicized shunt at Crystal Palace accounted for about £400 of that.

It was a good year, even though at times it was a bit frustrating. I got a couple of wins, and quite a lot of good places . . . My first international win came at Rouen, and that was a landmark.

That first Continental win at Rouen came in June, and Hunt's second in the Coupe de l'Avenir at Zolder in Belgium, while at Zandvoort he was leading when his engine failed. The year's tally may appear modest, but it was achieved in the face of difficulties which could well have soured the ambitions of a less determined man. Hunt recalls his problems after the Pau race:

Not only had we totally run out of money, but in common with some other teams our petrol had been stolen, syphoned out of the tanks when the cars were in the paddock overnight. We had no alternative but to acquire some by the same means, which turned out to be easier said than done. We discovered that most French cars had locking petrol caps, so we were creeping round on our hands and knees at night finding one car in ten without a locking cap, and one

A first-lap scene so typical of the heyday of Formula 3, with Hunt in a March leading the up-and-coming Roger Williamson and a jostling field into the first corner at London's Crystal Palace circuit

in ten of the rest with enough petrol in it to make it worthwhile . . . We finally got to le Havre after two days on the road with no food – that was bad – and when I got on the ferry I borrowed some money, then I hitchhiked home . . .

For 1971 a controversial new regulation called for all engine air (the air to mix with fuel to form a combustible mixture) to pass through a tiny 20 mm hole into an airtight plenum chamber, with the dual objective of restraining the power output of engines and making them more reliable. That season began and ended with Hunt being disqualified from a win at Oulton Park and a second place at Brands Hatch because the sealed airbox on his car was found to be leaking.

Because I had only got those two wins in 1970 I decided to go back into Formula 3 in 1971, while a lot of the guys like the Fittipaldis, Pace and Lauda had moved up – Emerson was actually in Formula 1. It seemed that by staying in Formula 3 I would be able to get good sponsorship, really get into the racing and clean up, then jump straight into Formula 1. But that March 713 was a disastrous car with a useless engine, and I had a really big struggle with it all the time.

In 1971 Dave Walker did what I hoped I could do: cleaned up. He always had a good car, but he really was incredible, virtually unbeatable. Even when he was at a disadvantage in a group, he would just steer out in front and salvage a win – he was amazing. Then he went into Formula 1, and I don't know what the hell happened to him, because nobody could drive a Formula 3 car that well and a Formula 1 car that badly*.

That was a year when hardly anything seemed to go right, when the earlier flair showed through only occasionally, and when the 'Hunt the Shunt' sobriquet became familiar. He was driving a works-supported March in a deal where he was 'taken under the

---

*Peter Warr of Lotus, the team Walker drove for in both formulae, was convinced that Walker's failing was simply that he tried to drive Formula 1 as he had a Formula 3 car.

Incident at Zandvoort in May 1971
Maskell and Hunt running side by side into the Tarzan curve, where that locking wheel was to make Maskell's line unpredictable. Wheels touched and the March flipped, skated along upside down, showering sparks, as the roll-over bar collapsed. The car slewed round as it hit the trackside sand, and came to rest with Hunt trapped. However, his head had been forced down between his legs in the cockpit and when marshalls eventually lifted the car after what seemed a lifetime, he scrambled out. His injuries were confined to damage to vertebrae, badly lacerated hands and bruising

wing' of the factory and supplied with a car. He did win at Montlhéry, Brands Hatch, the Crystal Palace and the Nürburgring, and in a race at Barcelona was leading the field by 90 seconds when a thunderstorm broke and he spun away his lead in a brush with the guard rails that damaged the radiators and caused overheating. There were several shunts, and at Zandvoort Hunt emerged unscathed from a massive accident when his March skated upside down for about a hundred yards.

The consensus of trackside opinion was that Hunt had perhaps suffered because less experienced drivers were able to mix it with the recognized quick drivers, that being in the nature of Formula 3. When he was able to break clear from scrambling packs, he was able to pull cleanly away, but his record was marred (as much by mechanical problems as by accidents, incidentally). The coming man in Formula 3 was Roger Williamson.

He cleaned up in 1972, and the fact that he had better cars doesn't detract from his driving. He still had to win, and he did his winning as Dave Walker had.

Despite his 1971 setbacks, Hunt started the new season with March again, leading an STP-backed works team. This was totally unsuccessful, and after an argument at Monaco he left the team (where his replacement was Jochen Mass, with whom he was to be teamed in 1976).

Hunt had retired after a first lap accident in his qualifying heat, when he was involved in somebody else's accident. In a typically forthright statement a few days later, he explained:

The fiasco at Monte Carlo was only the climax to a situation which has existed all year, stemming from a variety of problems caused basically by a lack of interest and enthusiasm. I made every effort to inject either interest or enthusiasm, without success. I now feel that the interests of my career would be better served by racing on my own.

Now a Falstaffian figure, described in a contemporary article as 'an eccentric British lord', appeared at British circuits, and at Thruxton James Hunt drove a Dastle for Lord Hesketh.

Anthony 'Bubbles' Horsley recalls that he had started talking with Lord Hesketh about a modest racing venture in 1971. 'He had decided to go motor racing, and our first idea was that I would buy a chassis and he would buy the engine, but it expanded rather quickly in the winter of 1971 and we thought in terms of a two-car team. I made an approach to James through a third party during the winter – I don't know if that ever actually reached him – then after he had his bust-up with March at Monte Carlo I jumped straight back in, and got him. His next move was some years later...' Horsley and Hunt discussed the possibility at Chimay, had two meetings in London and then finally reached agreement at a Mallory Park race meeting. The foundations for one of the most romantic episodes in recent racing had been laid.

The racing world was a little puzzled by this team. Its Dastles were 'clever' – neither inspired nor competitive – and to some its drivers seemed an odd pair: by this time a question mark hovered

over Hunt, while 'Bubbles' Horsley, erstwhile racer turned car-trade wheeler and dealer turned racing driver, somehow seemed to lack aptitude, to have problems keeping his cars 'on the island'. Crashes marred the progress of the team. In practice for the Formula 3 race at the British Grand Prix meeting at Brands Hatch, Hunt was closely following a Lotus which went out of control when a tyre punctured. He tried to spin to avoid it, but failed. His Dastle flipped twice and landed upside down on a safety barrier (fortunately one of the few strong points of the Dastle was its monocoque!). Horsley also crashed in practice, and the double setback brought the short life of the Hesketh Formula 3 team to an end.

That accident was Hunt's last in his Formula 3 career, save that when driving home from that meeting his Mini was involved in a road accident and the few days he spent in hospital postponed his Formula 2 debut.

By the end of that year, however, he had reaffirmed his old promise in Formula 2, rounding off 1972 with an excellent third place in the final British championship round at Oulton Park and, with renewed Hesketh backing, taking his March to races at Albi and Hockenheim – and finishing 'in the points'. Horsley, meanwhile, was to find his true racing metier as a team manager.

Nowadays Hunt keeps an eye on Formula 3, although not in a self- or team-imposed talent-spotting role. Looking back, he reflects: *It really was important, and although it went through a doldrums period, it has been returning to that role. Two things hurt it, the change in formula and the increase in costs. It became heavily inflated, to the point where a driver needed a lot of sponsorship to do it. The income that you could derive from Formula 3 became irrelevant weighed against the costs. We could soldier around Europe picking up £100 or so in start money and living on £20 between races – that was serious income. But then the costs became so great that those who had the sponsorship didn't mind whether they had income from races or not. So they did the domestic championship races for £25 prize money, and as these championships seemed to assume more importance the international circuit we had gone around really ceased to exist.*

After a disappointing final period in Formula 3, Hunt started to make a name for himself all over again in Formula 2, for example with an excellent drive at Oulton Park where he finished third behind the works cars driven by Niki Lauda and Ronnie Peterson after the rear wing had worked loose.

The Hesketh Years

Lord Hesketh and Anthony 'Bubbles' Horsley can take full credit for launching Hunt on his way to the world championship. For three years, Hesketh fielded Formula 1 cars for Hunt, who owes his chances to pursue the championship to the rich young man who started going racing for the pleasure of it and found himself embroiled in the business of grooming a Grand Prix star.

As Hunt the Shunt, James would in the normal course of events have been unemployable in Formula 1, where team managers prefer their drivers to be a little steadier in their approach. But it was not a normal team that was to employ James Hunt. After their disappointments in Formula 3, Hunt had persuaded Hesketh to provide an engine for a Formula 2 chassis borrowed from March; other friends helped, including one who came up with £1000 for tyres; Hunt and a mechanic ran the car. The March 712 was a year old, but Hunt showed that it could be competitive, and that he could overcome the handicap of a 1·8-litre engine when some of his competitors were using the full 2-litre power units permitted by the regulations. Some time later, Max Mosley was to wryly comment

Hunt on his way to a rewarding fifth place in the Rothmans 50,000 at Brands Hatch in 1972

'all of a sudden he was leading our works cars.'

A fifth place in the Rothmans 50,000 at Brands Hatch, and the good prize money that went with it, helped to get the team through the season, and before it ended Hesketh Racing as such was reformed. The plan for 1973 was to concentrate on Formula 2 and take in a few Formula 1 races, but as the season opened Formula 2 seemed only to offer the prospect of vain pursuit of the works March-BMWs.

Hesketh reasoned that rather than fooling around at the back of Formula 2 races, he might as well be running at the back of Formula 1 races for the same money. Once the team was into Formula 1, and there was a real prospect of getting some good results, other categories were quickly forgotten.

A Surtees TS9B which had not turned a wheel for four months was hired for the non-championship Race of Champions early in the season.

We lost a lot of time getting it to run properly, but if we had been able to run a full practice then there might have been a shock result. That car was a lot better than most people thought it was, and at Brands Hatch on Firestones it was really very good. I had to spend the first half of the race getting used to its power, and finding out about driving a Formula 1 car, otherwise we could have won.

Hunt's third place at Brands Hatch – at the line he was only inches behind Denny Hulme, who was giving the first McLaren M23 its first race in Europe – justified the venture into championship racing with a March 731. At Monaco the Hesketh equipe's playboy appurtenances – the 160 ft *Southern Breeze*, the Bell Jet Ranger heli-

First Formula 1 drive, in the 1973 Race of Champions

First Grand Prix –
the Hesketh Racing
March at Monaco
in 1973

copter, the Silver Shadow *et al* – fired up the general press, but more
to the point Hunt's Grand Prix debut was impressive. He qualified
the March for the ninth row of the grid, and was running sixth in
the closing laps of the race when the engine expired.

Hunt scored his first championship point when he finished sixth
in the French Grand Prix, he was fourth in the British Grand Prix,
third in the Dutch, seventh in the Canadian. At Watkins Glen for
the season's finale he finished a stirring second to Ronnie Peterson's
Lotus in the United States Grand Prix. In his first season, having
contested only seven of the 15 races, he had been on the winner's
rostrum twice (third in Holland and second in America) and was
eighth in the world championship with a total of 14 points. He also
ran in practice for the Italian Grand Prix but the car was damaged in

an incident and as no spares were available at Monza it was withdrawn before the race. This was the first of three seasons of learning, for Hunt and the Hesketh team.

Through the year the larger-than-life style of Hesketh Racing continued to fascinate, at times as an apparently flagrant intrusion into a Grand Prix world that had perhaps become too inward-looking. The marquee on the fringe of the Silverstone paddock, tables laden with silverware and guests attended with a formality unusual at the one-time airfield, the far from unobtrusive presence of the fair sex, the white jackets, striped with red and blue – the equipe seemed out of place in the world of professional racing, and proved to be a natural focus for gossip columnists, who otherwise would have found Silverstone a barren place. But under the veneer the team was taking its racing seriously, and as much to the point other teams were having to take Hesketh seriously. In 1973 at least, expenditure on the hardware of racing was reasonable – those 14 world championship points were probably gained at less cost than any scored by other teams – and Lord Hesketh's attitude was that he was a business man and his racing team would have to be a successful business. During the next year, however, this sound

That first Formula 1 season ended on a high note, when Hunt chased Ronnie Peterson to the flag in the US Grand Prix at Watkins Glen

guideline seemed to have been abandoned, or perhaps it was over-whelmed by patriotic euphoria, and during the third year the talk was of a need for sponsorship sums five times greater than expenditure in 1973 . . .

Since that first Formula 1 season, Hunt has started to concentrate on a race three days before practice actually starts – five days before the race is run – and he has also accepted the need for test sessions. *Testing is a necessary evil, but I would never shirk it because it is the means to the end. I want to win races, and in order to win races I have to test, so I go to test sessions with enthusiasm. But I have to work at the enthusiasm all the time, because I don't enjoy it. When I test, I drive as if I am qualifying and racing. I drive as fast as I can all the time – I'm in that habit, and I want to keep it going.*

Dr Harvey Postlethwaite

Designer Harvey Postlethwaite had joined Hesketh Racing from March, and through 1973 had progressively modified the team's

731 until their own first Hesketh 308 was ready early in 1974.

The original Hesketh was a pretty good workmanlike car, but it wasn't as competitive as, say, the McLaren. Therein lay the differences in results. I had to keep the sharp edges on my driving to do it justice as it was, but even if it had been quicker it definitely wasn't a race winning car. But that was very good training, driving a car that was not too good.

Through most of that summer of 1974 only two third placings, in Sweden and Austria, interrupted a depressing sequence of retirements. The two late-season races in North America saw the car substantially revised, and fortunes changing, as Hunt finished fourth in the Canadian Grand Prix, then third at Watkins Glen. Early in the year, however, there had been that first Formula 1 victory, in the non-championship International Trophy race at Silverstone – Hesketh's local circuit.

It was just a super day, and it was lovely to win in England. The fun was in celebrating it – we were all staying at Hesketh's house, and he had a lot of friends there as well as his family – but we were not really flattered in any way. We had no illusions. We knew it was not going to be like that in the Grands Prix, and when it turned out not to be we didn't get disappointed. We knew the moment we crossed the line that it wasn't a Grand Prix, so we sat back and enjoyed it for what it was – our first win, and a very popular one with the crowd, and therefore something to celebrate. It was a great day . . .

On the circuits, 1975 was the year that Hesketh Racing came good. Hunt finished in eight of the 14 championship races, scoring points every time he finished. The great day came in June, among

Three champions. Hunt leads Niki Lauda (Ferrari) and Emerson Fittipaldi (McLaren) in the 1975 International Trophy race at Silverstone

the sand dunes at Zandvoort. The track was wet as the race started, but within a few laps was drying. Hunt timed his stop to change to 'dry' tyres perfectly, diving into the pits as soon as the racing line was dry enough for slicks to give an advantage in getting the power down. Then through the final laps he held off persistent attacks by Niki Lauda. He forced boldly past slower cars but took no chances, calmly keeping the top driver of 1975 at bay on the European circuit traditionally best suited to Ferraris. The Hesketh pits exploded with joy.

Looking back at the closing stages of the race, Hunt recalled: *All I could do was get on with my own race and drive as fast as I could. There was no point in worrying about Niki because what was going to happen, would happen. If he caught me up, he caught me up. There was nothing I could do to stop that, except to drive as fast as I could and delay it as long as possible, then if his car was faster than mine on the straight and he got past me, it would have been my tough luck. With that in mind I pressed on normally, and the whole thing was settled.*

It was a breakthrough for me and the team. By that time we had done more than enough to have earned even a lucky victory – we had run in strong and unchallenged second place in more Grands Prix than most people, without the leader breaking down . . .

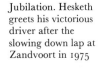

Jubilation. Hesketh greets his victorious driver after the slowing down lap at Zandvoort in 1975

My first Grand Prix win was obviously a personal breakthrough, and it killed two birds with one stone. It was run and won under the most extreme pressure from behind. Hitherto my most obvious weakness had been in leading races and running under pressure. I simply had no experience of doing it. If I

sat down in a room and talked about it, I could analyse it, but taking it with you on the track is another thing.

Formula 3 was the last racing I had done in a big way, and when you led in Formula 3 you were at a positive disadvantage – the others were swarming all over you. The Formula 3 races I had won had usually been last-lap slip-streaming spectaculars, where it was the luck of the draw who times it right in the dash for the line. So I had failed to realize that if you are in front in a Grand Prix you really have got the advantage.

Crossing the line first at Zandvoort improved my driving more than anything else, it rounded off my education, and I felt I could get on top of the others. When they are sitting behind you, then you can jolly well dictate your way of doing things.

In Argentina in 1977, Hunt was to reflect on two Hesketh episodes which he felt betrayed his inexperience. He qualified the Hesketh March for fifth place on the 1974 Argentine Grand Prix grid, made a storming start and actually took the lead from Ronnie Peterson part way through the opening lap:

I arrived at the hairpin in the lead, and unexpectedly clutchless. Quite frankly, it freaked me into a mistake. I got confused and overshot the hairpin. There was no clutch, I looked down for a moment, and off I went. It was a mistake of inexperience. I was over-excited at being in the lead – I had never led a Grand Prix before – and I was taken by surprise when the clutch went.

In the following year, he started from one place lower on the Argentine grid, and battled through to take the race lead from Carlos Reutemann's Brabham just before half distance. He led for

Soldiering on in the 308C at Monza, to a fifth place in the 1975 Italian Grand Prix

ten laps, with Emerson Fittipaldi pressing hard. Then he spun the Hesketh, and although he recovered and set a new lap record at just over 120 mph he was six seconds down in second place behind the McLaren at the flag.

I simply failed to cope with the pressure then, but you learn. Things like that are good background, the experience is a good basis for not doing it again, and you do become very conscious of it.

The Zandvoort race showed how thoroughly that weakness had been ironed out.

Despite increasing financial strains, the Hesketh team had a new car in the Silverstone paddock at the 1975 British Grand Prix. This 308C appeared lithe and low (it foreshadowed the disappearance of the tall air boxes above engines, which were to be outlawed in 1976), and it featured Aeon rubber springs all round in its suspension, these having earlier been tried in the front suspension by Hesketh Racing. This car gave the lie to the old adage 'what looks right, is right'. Hunt first raced it in the non-championship Swiss Grand Prix at Dijon (this French circuit had to be used as road racing has been banned in Switzerland since 1955). He placed it a lowly eighth, and struggled with it through the last two Grands Prix of the year, to fifth place at Monza and fourth at Watkins Glen, when the team felt that fine tuning would get it right.

It just didn't measure up to the 308B. The results that I did get with it were flattering both for me and for the car, and we achieved them by applying the lessons learned in the previous two years. We were in a bad situation with that car, which was not a good one, and we were getting the best we could out of it. Its performance did not reflect the speed of my driving so much as everything else we did in setting it up – all very subtle stuff. Whatever we did, it was definitely off the pace. A whole year later at Watkins Glen*, Jody had a go in it on the test day and he was quick, but only to the extent that I had been quick in it – not competitively quick, that is, but not right at the back as it had been all year. That showed that the car had remained pretty static.

That US Grand Prix at Watkins Glen was the last for Hesketh Racing, at least as a front-line team under the personal patronage of Lord Hesketh. In three short years it had become a very serious contender, the devil-may-care approach replaced by the professional pleasure of success in world championship racing. For the latter half of its life, however, it had been operating under increasingly threatening financial clouds.

I am sure that sponsorship could have been arranged, although not at the eleventh hour. We had known for 18 months that we probably would not make it to the end of 1975. I don't think that Alexander really wanted a sponsor – for very understandable reasons, he wanted it to stay as it had been, and as he was hoping to get things together in his business he didn't give sponsorship first priority.

When it became totally obvious that there was no other way, we had to get it through to a mind convinced that something else came first. When we did, it was too late. We could have got sponsorship. Bubbles could have gone out

---

* When it was being raced as a Wolf-Williams.

A characteristic
Hesketh pits scene,
with Alexander
watching from on
high

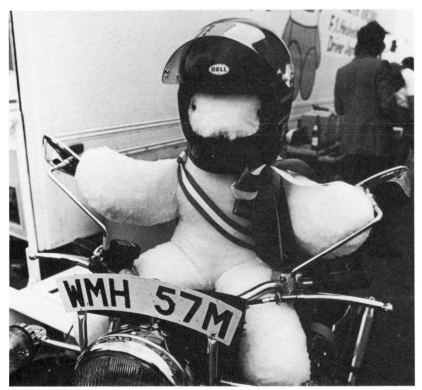

and got sponsorship (he is very good at that), and would have got it had he
been given the chance in June or July. But he was given more than assurances
that a serious effort was being made in London, he was given reasonable proof,
and as he was up in Towcester working 16 hours a day running the team and
trying to survive on a shoestring he didn't actually go down to London to check
it all out. Alexander had been saying that he was looking for a sponsor for a
year . . .

Horsley was to keep Hesketh Racing going at a secondary level
through 1976, using the older 308s, the 'one and three-quarter' 308Cs
which had been built in 1975 having been sold to Frank Williams.

Sad end. Lord
Hesketh accepts
a BARC award at
Thruxton from Lord
Howe, at what was
then assumed to be
the last appearance
of the Hesketh
team. However,
'Bubbles' Horsley
(extreme left) had
other ideas about
that . . .

The results achieved by this low-key operation in 1976 were modest – perhaps they showed just how good Hunt had been – but they were sufficient to keep the team in being as a springboard for 1977. Early in that year, Horsley was able to announce a new Hesketh, the 308E, and a more ambitious programme.

By the end of the 1975 season, however, the cost of staying afloat without a sponsor at the highest level in Formula 1 had become an impossibility for Lord Hesketh, who was forced to announce his withdrawal. It must have cost him close to £1 million to finance his Grand Prix programme, an expensive foundation for Hunt's world championship the following season in a Marlboro-McLaren.

We went through some bad patches at Hesketh Racing. Some of this was due to inexperience, some of it was bad luck coming all at once. Although I don't believe in luck in the long run, I do think it goes up and down in waves, and we suffered from this.

Bubbles taught me a lot. He taught me how to persevere and how to pull out of bad situations, and above all he taught me how to know myself better. I learned how to prepare for a race, and to always try to deliver a consistent performance. That is really one of the essential ingredients of success. Bubbles' criticism of my driving and my mental approach was always constructive.

Apart from Bubbles' tuition, I have to be grateful to Hesketh for the fact that I was training consistently all the time, on the limit. We thought it was a better car than it was, so there was no chance of relaxing, because if we were ever a little bit slow all heads turned to me. Driving in a car that is slightly uncompetitive teaches one to salvage points no matter what the circumstances, simply to make the best of a less than one hundred per cent situation.

I think now that could have made the difference between winning the championship in 1976 and finishing second. In three races, the McLarens were screwed up. Two I didn't finish, which was very lucky because they were both mechanical failures and we didn't get breakdowns at other times, but in the third I got two points in Sweden. I was very proud of that, because the car wasn't at all good – I reckon I drove one of my best races of 1976 in Sweden, simply keeping the thing on the island and going at a reasonable speed. That came from lessons learned in the hard times.

Manufactured Luck

The Chinese call it 'joss', the good fortune without which no successful business can expect to prosper. Racing teams tend to believe that luck is manufactured. From the outside, it appeared that the marriage of James Hunt with the McLaren team was pure 'joss', a chance of a lifetime with Emerson Fittipaldi leaving the team in the lurch at the end of the season and Britain's white hope, James Hunt, also ditched when the Hesketh team pulled out. It was not quite as simple as that. Through the autumn, the racing world had known that Fittipaldi had yet to renew his contract with McLaren.

Hunt did not feel that he was out on a limb towards the end of 1975, for although the Hesketh team was sinking fast for want of a sponsor, he had several alternatives.

There was no question of not getting into a car, it was a question of getting into a good car, getting the right drive. The main offers came from Brabham and Lotus.

On reflection, Hunt thinks that Brabham boss Bernie Ecclestone was trying to help him out of his difficulty by setting up a deal whereby James would drive Ford Cosworth powered Brabhams of the type raced by the works' team in 1975, while contracted Martini-Brabham drivers Carlos Pace and Carlos Reutemann drove the new BT45 cars powered by Alfa Romeo flat-12 engines. *But that would have been a difficult deal . . . I think Bernie was only doing it as a matter of generosity to me.*

The discussions with Lotus barely left the ground:

I had difficulty talking any sense to them at all. They seemed to be of the opinion that their drivers shouldn't be paid. The meeting with Lotus comprehensively wasted three hours of my life. They didn't even buy me lunch – we went out to lunch, but didn't get any. That left me out looking for lunch in London at 4 o'clock on a Sunday afternoon.

But Hunt knew that Fittipaldi had not signed his contracts with McLaren and Marlboro. *I didn't know why, and neither did they, but they smelled a rat and we all kept in touch.* It was agreed that if the Hesketh team did go under, Hunt was to give McLaren and Marlboro a full chance of putting a deal together. It transpired that Hunt was tipped off about Fittipaldi's decision three days before an announcement was made.

I knew before the team, because as one colleague to another Emerson told me before he told them. Domingos* called from Geneva – Emerson was in Brazil – on a Thursday afternoon, and the story broke on Saturday morning. He simply told me that Emerson would not be signing, not what he was going to do, just

---

* Domingos Piedade, Fittipaldi's business manager.

The old and the new. Hunt with 'Bubbles' Horsley and Teddy Mayer shortly after leaving Hesketh Racing and signing for Marlboro-McLaren

that he was leaving McLarens. That was a fine gesture by Emerson and Domingos; from a business point of view it gave me warning, time to get myself ready because at that point it was obvious that McLaren would need me. I had been in touch with McLaren for two months, purely on the basis: Emerson hasn't signed a contract – let's keep in touch. I knew that if Emerson didn't sign I was going to McLaren, and I had known that since the beginning of September.

McLaren team manager Teddy Mayer was thunderstruck when Fittipaldi told him he was leaving, although he had been aware that the Brazilian had been having problems towards the end of the 1975 season, partly because of pressure from his family and from Brazil to team up with his brother Wilson in their own organization and drive their Copersucar car. The way Mayer tells the story, he heard from Fittipaldi at 7 o'clock in the evening, and five minutes later was on the telephone to Hunt – 'I barely stopped to say goodbye to Emerson before I got onto James and asked if he would drive for us. Within 36 hours we had concluded a deal.'

The same night Hunt arranged a sponsorship deal with John Hogan, responsible for Marlboro racing activities, and by the following evening they had shaken hands on a contract. Hogan was later to say that Hunt must have been the cheapest world champion in recent racing history. The deal they agreed that Sunday evening might have solved Hunt's immediate financial problems to his satisfaction, but when he signed a contract for the 1977 and 1978 seasons after clinching the world title in Japan, it was for nearly five times the amount of the 1976 fee.

Right: Hunt holding off Niki Lauda in the closing laps of the 1975 Dutch Grand Prix

48

Specification
Engine: Ford-Cosworth DFV V8; bore and
stroke 85·7 × 64·8 mm; capacity 2993 cc;
max power 465 bhp at 10,500 rpm.
Transmission: McLaren-modified Hewland
FG400 six-speed gearbox.
Suspension: Front: double wishbones,
inboard coil spring/damper units, anti-

roll bar. Rear: parallel lower links and single top link mounted on tubular cross beam, twin radius rods, outboard coil spring/damper units.

Wheels: 13 in diameter magnesium, 10 in wide (front) and 18 in wide (rear) rims. Goodyear tyres.

Brakes: Lockheed 10 in diameter disc, outboard at front, inboard at rear.

Steering: McLaren rack and pinion.

Principal dimensions: wheelbase, 105·75 in to April 1976, subsequently 107 in; front track, 65 in; rear track, 66·5 in to May 1976, subsequently 65·5 in; approx weight, 1,325 lb.

The McLaren M23 in its 1976 form. Basically it was a straightforward design, adaptable and simple to adjust for most circuits. By 1976 standards it was a long-wheelbase, wide-track car. In this drawing, the oil coolers are mounted ahead of the rear wheels rather than under the rear wing.

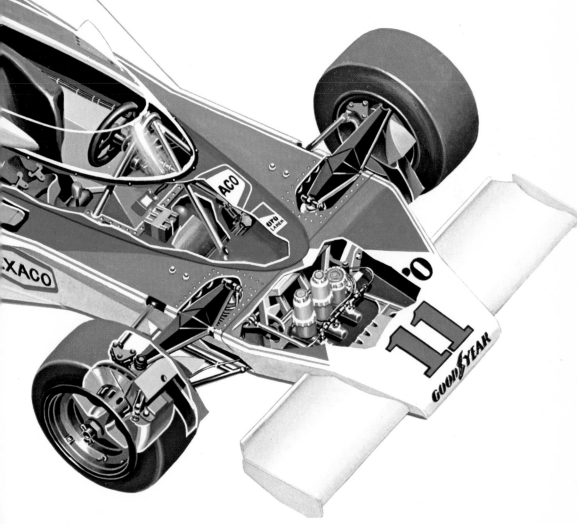

Hunt had been impressed by the McLaren record, rating it as perhaps the most consistent team of the 1970s, *but in terms of winning, of course there were other teams that were a little better.* He was impressed by the M23, the car designed by Gordon Coppuck back in 1972, as a derivative of the M16, which had been the pace-setter at Indianapolis since it first ran there in 1971. It had been painstakingly developed, and raced with distinction for four seasons, an unusually long front-line life for a Grand Prix design.

The M23 appeared angular, but had excellent aerodynamic properties (**left**). **Below:** Hunt in the car for the first time, flanked by Mayer and Caldwell

The M23 had gone particularly well in the latter part of the 1975 season, although there really didn't seem to be anything special about it. Emerson hadn't really given Niki Lauda a hard time. He gave chase at Monza and at Watkins Glen in the United States Grand Prix, but that was really about all. However, I was pleased that it should be the best car apart from Ferrari.

Ferrari was perhaps the only other team Hunt would really have wanted to join – indeed, there were rumours of a flirtation in the summer of 1976 – although he was later to say that he would have driven a Ferrari only if it was run by the McLaren team.

Once the deal was done, Hunt wondered how he would be received by a team he hardly knew apart from nods in the pit lanes, and how his new sponsors might react to his casual style. Jeans and a tee shirt were his normal dress, and the prospect of donning the Marlboro team's blazer, tie and tailored flannels appalled him.

I told them when I was signing the contract that they could take out the clause about the uniform, because I wasn't going to wear it. I sincerely believed that it would be better for them to let me be my natural self, in terms of publicity and everything else, than if they dressed me up like a Philip Morris cigarette carton, and they said 'OK. Fine'.

Paradoxically, about the only thing not casual about Hunt is his defence of the casual manner in which he dresses. He feels that his life is regulated enough without having to dress to instructions as well. *It's really the principle of the thing, to do what I want to do whenever I can. Life is too short to be bound by regulations when it isn't absolutely essential.*

He expounds an unconvincing theory about not carrying a jacket when he travels because the constant folding and packing would ruin it before he ever got around to wearing it. Now that he has the championship, will he become a little more formal? It's a sore point. He maintains he has always dressed with respect to whatever he has been doing.

I mean, I'm not going to turn up in a tee shirt at Buckingham Palace, but I don't plan on making any undue changes and I don't think anyone will be asking me to. The only changes will probably be that I'll attend more formal functions than before and I'll dress accordingly.

As it turned out, the team did work well together, and one key to their cohesion was the fact that they were all, at around 30, of much the same age. Hogan too established a rapport with Hunt because he had grown up with racing and racing people, knows when not to 'make waves', and knows when to make them most effectively. Hunt respects the straight approach, and this has stood him in good stead in the understanding company of his racing partners; his tendency to give direct expression to his feelings and opinions was to have less happy effects during the third Grand Prix of 1976 at Long Beach.

When I came to McLarens I was equipped to operate on my own, which is what you have to do when you are with McLaren – they don't expect to have to teach a driver anything. So I was very fortunate that I was still with Hesketh in 1975, as I probably learned more in that year than in any other about how to prepare myself for a race and then deliver at the weekend. Thick or thin.

The Car

The McLaren M23 has been one of the outstanding Grand Prix cars of the 1970s, competitive from the day it was introduced in 1973 through to 1977 and driven to two world championships, by Emerson Fittipaldi in 1974 and James Hunt in 1976.

Basically the design, which followed widely-accepted lines when it was introduced, is straightforward and uncomplicated, and proved to have unusual development potential. Although its predecessor, the M19, was hardly approaching obsolescence in 1972, revised regulations due to come into effect in 1973 seemed to require that it should be replaced; a prime requirement of those revised rules was that the fuel system had to be protected against crash damage, and as far as the tanks were concerned this meant encasing them in a 'deformable structure' allowing for a 'crushable' and fire-resistant absorbing layer which in some areas is as much as four inches thick.

The M23 was designed by McLaren's chief designer Gordon Coppuck, who appears to be out of the quiet bespectacled 'boffin'

Pits lane conference with designer Gordon Coppuck

mould – in fact, in the mid-1960s he was a top competitor in International Six Days Trial motorcycle events. He is the only man at McLaren Racing with a 'technical' academic qualification. He had joined McLaren from the National Gas Turbine Establishment, and when Robin Herd left (to design the never-to-be-raced Cosworth four-wheel drive GP car and then become one of the founders of March) Coppuck was largely responsible for the immensely successful M8 sports-racing cars. Discussing the M23, he recalls 'The M23 was conceived as a replacement for the M19, largely because of the deformable structure regulations. We could have added a deformable structure to the M19, but it would have been difficult and in any case in the nature of a bolt-on effort just to meet the regulations. We followed the spirit as well as the letter of these in building the M23 round a fully-integral deformable structure.

'We chose a square profile rather than the round one of the M19 simply for aerodynamic reasons. In a modern racing car, aerodynamic efficiency does not depend on a streamlined shape, like a pre-war land speed record car, but on getting the aerofoils to work properly. Through the life of the car one of the main changes has been in the wheelbase, which has been extended from 101 inches to almost 108 inches, and this has had the effect of moving the rear wing further back from the engine, which helps increase the amount of downforce which it generates. The car was right down to the weight limit when we started racing it, and although it has got a little heavier we have generally kept the weight problem in hand – the

Hunt marked the fifth anniversary of the introduction of the M23 by taking pole position for the 1977 South African GP, and leading the race despite the fact that the car lacked straight-line speed compared with some later designs. Here he heads Lauda, Scheckter and the rest of the field into the first corner, Crowthorne

air starter we introduced in 1976 has helped in this respect. The longer wheelbase has also made the car easier to handle near the limit on most circuits, although it is a handicap at Monaco where the car has perhaps been least effective (we did build a short-wheelbase version for Monaco 1974, but it was not successful).

'The major change in 1976 was the six-speed gearbox, which Alastair Caldwell had started working on in the winter of 1974–75, and had fully developed for 1976. The advantage of this is that the engine can be kept in the most effective rev band, within about 2000 rpm – the DFV can match the Ferrari engine on straights, but not in all-round torque, and our objective with the six-speed box was to make the most of the useful engine speed range.

'Throughout 1976 James drove M23/8/2, which was built in 1975 and first raced by Emerson in that non-championship Swiss Grand Prix at Dijon.

With us, James has been a very considerate driver – he doesn't bounce the car over kerbs very often, for example – and he responds very well to handling changes. We have not been a pole position team in the past (one of the few times was when Denny put the M23 on pole for its first race, and that was his first-ever pole in an F1 car), so we were highly delighted when James started with us by getting pole position in Brazil. And several times since then . . .

'We normally build a car for a two-year racing life – one year sorting out, one year when it is really competitive. A third year is a bonus, and we were therefore delighted with the extra bonus we had with the M23, world championships in 1974 and 1976, runner-up in 1975'.

In passing, the Ford-Cosworth DFV engine used by McLaren and by most other Grand Prix teams is even more remarkable than the M23, for it first powered a winning Formula 1 car in 1967 – the year before James Hunt started driving single-seater racing cars. Cosworth rated the DFV output at 465 bhp at 10,500 rpm in 1976, but there are usually slight variations between identical-specification engines, and attention to detail by Nicholson McLaren Engines, in preparation and aspects such as the exhaust, could produce a little more power.

Hunt has a high regard for the team, and the car (see page 53). Even his critics frequently had to concede that his driving was impeccable, and he took every advantage of the speed which the M23 had shown in late 1975, when earlier in that season it had begun to seem that it might be losing its competitive edge.

Once a flag has dropped, though, he is a competitor first and foremost, and although he does not ill-use his machinery, it becomes very much a means to an end:

Basically, the instruments are pretty irrelevant in a race – if you are busy racing hard in the middle of a pack and the water temperature goes up it's tough shit. You can't get out and blow on the radiator, you might as well ignore it and run until the engine blows up. If you lose oil or you lose oil pressure in practice it is good to realize it, because you might be able to catch it – except that by the time the pressure has dropped in the line the engine might have

Components such as
brakes have to be
bedded in, and
mechanics obviously
feel that even the
best of drivers might
be forgetful . . .

blown anyway! Occasionally in a race you can look at the instruments and act accordingly – in Argentina in 1977 I happened to be miles in the lead and cruising, so there I could drive to match the fact that the water was hotter than I would have liked it to be.

As far as possible, I have a look round the car during a race, but really I only look for things if I think there is something wrong. I can't check – say – the rear tyres because of the way I have my mirrors set. (I like them so that I can see everything outside the car, and provided I look at the right moment, when the cockpit surround isn't vibrating so that you can't see anything but a blur, I can see what I need to.)

He is safety conscious, about all aspects of racing, but he disagrees with the regulations – and with general opinion – in one respect.

Since the freak incident in Argentina in 1977, when the on-board fire extinguisher on Mario Andretti's JPS exploded during practice for the Grand Prix, he has regarded these devices as potentially dangerous. At Buenos Aires he asked Mayer to either remove the extinguisher bottle from his M23, or at least empty it, but Mayer told him that the regulations stipulate that the bottle be carried, and be in working order, or the car would risk disqualification. On the M23 the extinguisher bottle is tucked snugly under the driver's legs – if it had been Hunt's extinguisher that had exploded it would have torn his legs off . . .

I think we would be better off without fire extinguishers on the cars. They can't cope with a major fire, the only thing they can handle is a small electrical fire, and if you've got one of those you might as well climb out of the car. I suppose you could have an electrical fire when you were trapped in a car after an accident, and it would put that out, but I have never heard of it happening. I reckon they are more of a hazard than they are worth.

Meticulous attention to detail has always been a McLaren hallmark. And 'detail' in a racing car can encompass a wider range than many spectators might imagine. For example, maintaining driver effectiveness through races in great heat can be a problem, and carrying liquid refreshment for a driver in a Grand Prix car is a supremely simple operation of enormous complexity. The bottle has to be mounted in such a way, and the tube installed carefully, so that the liquid does not advance and retreat under conditions of acceleration and braking. The drinking tube has to be piped up inside the driver's helmet, through a hole in his fireproof balaclava and into his mouth, where he has to keep it clenched between his teeth throughout the race (if it slips out, the driver suddenly has an enormous problem, as there is no way he can get it back unaided and it can drench him in liquid). During 1976 the McLaren team had experimented with a bottle in an attempt to cope with a problem peculiar to Hunt, a feeling of nausea every time he had built up a safe lead and his body relaxed slightly; if he had something to drink, it was thought it might cure his uncomfortable urge to retch. *Whenever the pressure was off, I had a sort of release in tension, as though my body was physically loosening up, and although I was never actually sick I was dry-retching. Whenever I get a clear lead and am driving to finish as opposed to racing, the same thing happens. We thought that if I could wet my mouth during the race it might help to cure the problem, so we experimented with a bottle during practice for the German Grand Prix. The plan was that I would take a drink on the straight at the Nürburgring, the only place I had time, and then blow back down to the bottle until I could feel it bubbling and the line was clear. At the Nürburgring you're doing 180 mph on the straight and then the track goes wiggle-wiggle-wiggle-BRAKE, and you are as busy as you will ever be in a racing car. Right in the middle of the busiest bit a half pint of orange juice came straight in my face! The whole bloody lot! Up the tube and all over the place. We carried out a series of experiments after that, but we never did get it exactly right. I still have to sit there for half the bloody race chewing on the tube with my tongue over the end of it . . .*

The McLaren mechanics find a moment to relax at Mosport in 1976. **Left to right:** Lance Gibbs (back to camera), Mark Scott, Steven Bunn, Dave Ryan, Ray 'Kojak' Grant; behind car, 'Hampton McLaren' Howard Moore, Hunt's chief mechanic throughout the season

The 1976 Line Up

Grand Prix racing is a technically sophisticated sport, wholly in tune with the 1970s, and a thoroughly international sport. Championship races are held in many parts of the free world, some long-established – the French Grand Prix was first run in 1906 – others such as the race at Long Beach in California very new.

Until 1976 each country was allowed only one championship race in a year, but the United States laid claim to two because of its vast geographical size, and in 1976 for the first time a US Grand Prix West was run at Long Beach as well as the traditional US Grand Prix at Watkins Glen in upstate New York. There are championship races in Argentina and Brazil, South Africa, Canada and Japan, as well as the European races in Spain, Belgium, Monaco, Sweden, France, Britain, Germany, Austria, Holland and Italy.

The backdrops for the circuits are often excitingly national. In Italy the Monza track is laid out in the grounds of a one-time royal park on the outskirts of Milan, the track in Japan is at the foot of Mount Fuji, the Osterreichring in Austria is set in picturesque Alpine foothills, and the street race at Long Beach is across the harbour from the permanent mooring of the *Queen Mary*, while the Monaco Grand Prix is run through the streets of the tiny Principality.

The Grand Prix line-up changes from year to year. Some teams always seem to be contenders, and have been for decades, while others come and go. Drivers and other personnel change too, but once they do make a change they tend to stay with a team for more than one season.

In general conception, modern Grand Prix cars conform to a pattern, partly because of the international regulations but generally because of the common answer to the challenge of building the ultimate machines for one specific purpose – getting round a variety of road courses as quickly as possible.

All cars are built round a monocoque, an immensely strong metal tub that houses fuel cells holding around 40 gallons of petrol and protects the driver, who 'sits' in a reclining position. Engines are invariably mounted between the driver and the rear wheels, with the transmission and gearbox grouped at the rear. A prominent aerofoil 'wing' at the rear can be adjusted to provide degrees of negative lift, or 'downforce', which helps steady a car through fast corners and under braking. The 'wing' on a racing car has the reverse effect to wings on an aircraft – on a racing car, the wing section is 'upside down' so that the airstream forces the vehicle down rather than up. The amount of downforce can be regulated by changing the angle of the rear wing, while front to rear balance is altered by adjustment of the smaller wings on either side of the nose.

Aerodynamic balance – tuning the shape of the car to make the best use of the airstream passing over it – has to be calculated extremely carefully during practice sessions. Too much angle on the rear wing means adequate downforce, but at the expense of extra 'drag'; with a shallow angle on the wing the car will be faster on straights but less stable in corners. The accuracy of the 'balancing act' during practice is one mark of an experienced driver.

Most Grand Prix cars in the 1970s have used the Ford-Cosworth DFV engine, an eight-cylinder unit with its cylinders in 'vee' formation. Ferrari use a 12-cylinder engine, with its cylinders in two horizontally opposed banks of six, and known as a 'flat 12'. By comparison, the Matra engine in the French Ligier is a 12-cylinder unit in vee formation, a V-12.

Many cars have the name of their principal sponsor linked with the name of their constructor; hence Hunt's car in 1976 was a Marlboro-McLaren because of a major sponsorship by Philip Morris, parent company of the Marlboro cigarette brands, of the McLaren team. The Elf-Tyrrells are so named because the team owner, Ken Tyrrell, negotiated a sole sponsorship deal with the French Elf oil company when he first went Formula 1 racing with Jackie Stewart as his number one driver in 1968. John Player Specials are Lotus cars, under the black and gold cigarette-packet livery. Until 1977 the proud Ferrari team did not bear outward signs of sponsorship on its cars, although it received huge financial backing from the Fiat group in Italy.

New Beginning
Brazil and South Africa

Between signing the contract with McLaren and the first race of the 1976 season in Brazil in mid-January, Hunt had very little contact with his new team, apart from two abortive test sessions at Silverstone, curtailed by poor weather, and a seat-fitting session at the McLaren factory, which also turned out to be a waste of time.

A driver is effectively designed into his racing car, and he has to FIT – if he moves from side to side, or slides up and down in the reclining seat even half an inch, the strain can become intolerable during the length of a race, and as it becomes intolerable so his effort can be affected. So the seat fitting becomes every bit as important as being measured for a Savile Row suit.

The big problem is that when you sit in a car in the workshop you can get everything roughly right, but there's no way you can get it exactly right until you reach the racetrack. When we got to Brazil it was all wrong, of course. It didn't fit me, the steering was too heavy and I didn't like it, so the first day of practice was spent getting the car right for me to drive, and we did nothing at all towards getting the car set up and sorted out for the circuit.

Hunt reflects that because the intention of the team was to pension off the M23 early in the season and bring in the new M26, they did not really persevere to get the M23 cockpit exactly right. Simply to accommodate Hunt's gangly length in a car built for the considerably shorter Fittipaldi they had to cut into the front bulkhead and mount the pedals ahead of it instead of behind it.

Before that vital first race with his new team, the first day of practice was lost fitting Hunt into his car. The following day the engine blew up during the first session. By the time a replacement DFV had been installed the final practice session had already started. With 20 minutes left, Hunt motored out on to the circuit at Interlagos, 5 miles of dips and twists which over the 200-mile Grand Prix distance make it a very hard track. There was no time left for fancy mechanical settings: it was down to the driver. Hunt responded to the situation, aware that his new team would measure him for the rest of the season against his performance in the few laps he could put in. He gathered pace in spectacular fashion, and to his own and his team's delight wound up taking pole position. The fairy tale had started.

That first pole position of Hunt's Grand Prix career was significant in a number of ways, among them the fact that he had used Brazilian Emerson Fittipaldi's 1975 car to take pole position in Fittipaldi's 'home' Grand Prix. This did not go unnoticed in the McLaren camp, where memories still smarted from the former champion's last-minute desertion. *It was also important psychologically because we immediately had each other's confidence and respect.* Hunt took full advantage of the situation to establish his 'normal way of behaviour', the casual style, *which was not what they had been used to with Emerson. If you behave 'badly' in terms of what is traditionally good behaviour, nobody minds when you are doing well . . . but as soon as you are not doing well they point the finger at you and say 'that's the reason'.*

For his first race in the M23 he was to start alongside the acknowledged master, Niki Lauda, who had qualified his Ferrari just two hundredths of a second slower. Lauda was regarded by Hunt with a mixture of awe and some respect. Hunt's attitude of the moment explains another of his strong beliefs:

The most important thing in life is to know yourself and know your limitations. While I felt confident that I could do the job I am trying to do – by which I mean be the best – I hadn't done it then, so I had no right to feel that I could. And at that level you can only hope that you are right.

Throughout his Formula 1 career Hunt had been in the one-car team created around him and for him by Lord Hesketh. Although he had won that 1975 Dutch Grand Prix, and won it well, early in 1976 he could not be sure how well he had been driving that particular Hesketh, because there were no performances by another driver to use as a yardstick. His younger brother and business manager, Peter, remembers being worried at that stage. Nobody really knew how good James was. 'Maybe the Hesketh was a super

First race of the season, with Lauda surging ahead of pole position driver Hunt at Interlagos. Regazzoni on the left, Jarier and Fittipaldi following

car and his driving was only average.' James analysed the position:
If you want to be ridiculous about it, I wasn't to know if the Hesketh was a car that was three seconds a lap better than anything else and I was just driving it slowly, or vice versa – that it was three seconds a lap worse than anything else and I was driving it mighty quick. You can form opinions, but you don't know for sure.

Privately, he felt that if he got into the right car he would start winning. But that is the sort of thing a driver does not tell the world until he is winning.

Lauda made the best start at Interlagos, snatching the advantage of pole position away from Hunt. This was to happen several times in the season, as Hunt lived with his fear of burning out his clutch with startline heroics. A mediocre driver can make poor starts in the middle of a grid and these will go unnoticed, swallowed in the tyre smoke and excitement. But when a driver makes poor starts from the front row of a grid he has to have an explanation, because the whole world is his critic.

The most important thing to consider in a start is the clutch. I've burned two clutches in my Formula 1 career, and I've seen other people burn clutches at the start, and do it more than once. The second time I ruined a clutch I vowed that I would never do it again. You can beat everybody off the line by slipping the clutch. But that is plain stupid if it means you are last after 50 yards because your clutch continues to slip and everybody has gone past. So while I have always wanted to make good starts – and tried to – I err on the side of safety, because one thing I don't want to do is not get to the first corner at all. I would rather be third there than walking back to the pits . . .

Lauda made up four or five seconds on Hunt, following his Ferrari team mate Clay Regazzoni, who had made one of his sling-shot starts from the second row, and he stayed in front of the McLaren driver when Regazzoni slipped down the order with a puncture. Two-thirds of the way through the race there was a freak failure on Hunt's engine. One of the fuel injector trumpets fell off, taking with it the inbuilt injector nozzle, and in effect turning the Ford-Cosworth V-8 into a seven-cylinder engine. In spite of this Hunt thought that he might be able to soldier on into third or fourth place. Then the errant trumpet fell down behind the throttle slides, jamming the throttle open, and Hunt speared off into the catch fencing. He got his car back on to the track, but the rear-mounted oil coolers had been dragged off, so he parked and watched Lauda cruise on to win comfortably, by more than 20 seconds from Patrick Depailler in the Elf-Tyrrell.

As he left Brazil Hunt was not entirely despondent. He had out-paced the field in practice and he had kept pace with Lauda in the race. The freak problem which had parked him was outside his con-trol, and was therefore disregarded. In himself, Hunt knew he had what it took. All he needed was the chance.

People get a winning streak, and that's what happened to us in the second part of the 1976 season. I said early in the year, right after South Africa, that the title would obviously be between Niki and myself because we were both so evenly matched, but the scales were in his favour then because he was on a winning streak. He had been winning in the previous year, and he carried on. It just needed something to tip those scales, to end his winning streak, and we would be winning.

Early charger Vittorio Brambilla dives inside Mass in the braking area at the end of the main straight at Kyalami, while Hunt stays warily behind them as the group pursues race leader Lauda

At Kyalami for the South African Grand Prix Hunt had again been on pole, by a tenth of a second from Lauda. But when the start light flashed green Lauda was gone, rear tyres wreathed in smoke as the 500 horsepower of the Ferrari flat-12 blasted the Austrian into an immediate lead on the long swooping run to the first right-hander. On that first lap Hunt was fourth, paying for his tardiness off the line with an early-laps battle with the hard-charging

Vittorio Brambilla in the Beta March. Hunt's team mate Jochen Mass soon gave way to the pair of them and Hunt forced past Brambilla. But although he could pace Lauda from a distance in second place, he could not close appreciably until the race entered its closing phase. Then Hunt's pit signal board showed that the gap to the Ferrari was shrinking. Hunt piled on the pressure, and the gap between the Ferrari and the McLaren when the chequered flag came out was down to 1·3 seconds. Lauda's car had a softening rear tyre, which slowed him marginally and reduced his lead over Hunt, but the result was indicative of the way the season would go. James Hunt's determined drive in this GP showed Lauda and Ferrari that Fittipaldi's replacement in the McLaren team was a man to be reckoned with.

The Fuse is Lit
California and Spain

A world championship Grand Prix round the streets of Long Beach, California, was the improbable dream and inspiration of an expatriate Englishman named Christopher Robin Pook. At first there were doubts that Pook's organization could raise the money to mount a race, but they did. It was a complicated arrangement involving the City fathers of Long Beach, who were keen to promote their town internationally. Pook set up a race for Formula 5000 cars in 1975 to establish his concept of Californian street racing and so provide the venue for a World Championship Grand Prix in 1976. There were further doubts that the track through city streets could be made safe enough to satisfy the drivers, but it was. It was just over two miles in length, with the main straight powering between cinemas (showing pornographic movies) and fading hotels, one of which was to burn down during the 1976 race. The promoters were keen to present the event as echoing the round-the-houses style of the Grand Prix at Monaco. There were Press references to Monaco as 'Long Beach East'. The Californian race had been titled U.S. Grand Prix (West).

The Marlboro-McLaren team squared up for the third round of the championship with Hunt fresh from a win in the Race of Champions at Brands Hatch. Long Beach would be his first race with the M23 on a slow track, and he was unsure of his chances because the car had never been particularly good on tight, slow tracks. In practice, however, he was pleasantly surprised and qualified third fastest for the race behind Regazzoni (Ferrari) and Depailler (Elf-Tyrrell), with Lauda beside him on the second row. It was the first time he had missed pole position, but three tenths of a second covered the first three cars and Hunt was satisfied that come the race he could handle his opponents.

It was one of those practice sessions where everyone was getting quicker all the time and we were as good as anybody. The four of us had been fast, swapping times, and there was really nothing to choose between us. My car had gone well on full tanks and we were in great shape.

The weight of the fuel load makes a difference to the balance of the car. On the starting grid the car is carrying around 40 gallons of fuel and as the race progresses and this load is used up, so the balance of the car changes. Early in the race the drivers have to make allowances in their braking distances, for instance, taking into account the extra weight on the car. As the fuel load decreases, they are able to drive harder.

I made a good start in the race for a change, passed Depailler, and set off on

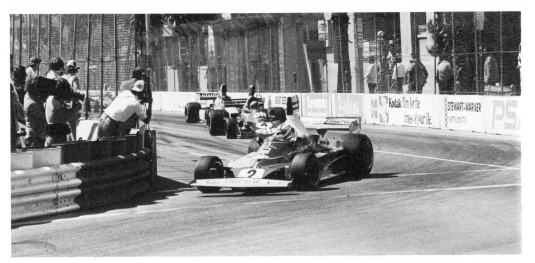

The streets of Long Beach. Race-winner Regazzoni heads Depailler and Hunt, who were to tangle dramatically on the fourth lap

the opening lap second behind Regazzoni. It was looking good. Then as I left the hairpin on to the straight my engine died . . . it just faded away for what must have been three seconds, and then picked up again, but by that time Depailler was alongside and gone. It was a vapour lock in the fuel system, something that happens for no good reason that anyone can find, just after you switch off the electric fuel pump*.

It cost me second place to Depailler and put me in a position a few laps later that I need not have been in if it hadn't been for the engine dying. Ever since then I've switched the electric pump off before the start and kept the revs up. It's a risk because the mechanical pump doesn't work under 3000 rpm, it doesn't produce enough fuel pressure, and the engine can stall. But on balance it's safer than having the engine die out on the track.

On the third lap, Depailler went wide on a corner and presented Hunt with the chance to move in on the attack.

I came up alongside him on the bottom straight, to his left with the pair of us heading into the right-hand hairpin which in the normal way with most people would have been a perfectly normal, reasonable manoeuvre. He had the inside line for the hairpin so I couldn't pass him, but what I could do was to make him go into the corner very tight so that I could get a good line through and pass him on the straight coming out. I was trying to restrict his freedom of movement round that corner, to slow him and give myself a run at him on the straight. The mistake I made was failing to pull out my file which I keep mentally on every driver and how they behave, because with most other people this wouldn't have been a problem. But Patrick doesn't worry about things like that, and he moved over and just pushed me off the track on the straight and into the wall VERY HARD. So that was the end for me. It made me very cross.

At the time Hunt leapt from his car, fuse lit and blazing, and waited for Depailler to come round on the next lap, standing out in the track to shake his fist at the little Frenchman. For several laps he worked out his frustration like this, saying later that it wasn't

---

*Cars usually start a race with the electric fuel pump switched on to feed the engine until it is running hard enough for the mechanical fuel pump to take over.

dangerous because he was in full control for the situation. *The linear speed of a car is high but its directional speed is very low. I could have dodged a car quite easily if anyone had come close.*

Regazzoni and Lauda enjoyed an easy first and second respectively in the Ferraris, with Depailler third. At the press conference afterwards, Hunt appeared and started to press questions on Depailler about the accident. Things started to get heated, much to the delight of the Californian sportswriters, who were finding this action much more to their taste than trying to extract colourful comment from either of the Ferrari drivers. As a result Hunt emerged from Long Beach with the biggest press, but most of it was bad. However much he defends his behaviour during this episode, it marked a low point for him.

Nevertheless, as he left California Hunt was aware that he was still competitive and quite capable of winning a Grand Prix given a change in luck. As if to tantalize the team, back in Britain Hunt won the non-championship Silverstone Formula 1 race named in honour of the former world champion, Graham Hill, who had been killed when his private plane crashed, while returning from a test session in France at the end of 1975. The McLaren team was winning races, but it wasn't winning the right ones.

In Spain for the fourth round at Jarama, in Hemingway Civil War country outside Madrid, a new problem arose that Hunt had perhaps not encountered before. His German team mate Jochen Mass was emerging as a steady points earner, if not a pace-maker, and as the team went to Jarama, Mass was fourth in the championship with seven points, and Hunt was fifth with six. While Hunt had been flashing up pole positions and making the front running in the opening races, Mass, who had joined the McLaren team towards the end of the 1974 season, had actually overhauled Hunt with points gained from a sixth place in Brazil, a third in South Africa and a fifth in Long Beach. It had been generally assumed outside the team that Hunt had been taking Fittipaldi's place as Number One driver and title-chaser while the reliable Mass rode shotgun to keep the Ferraris away. Going down to Madrid, Mass didn't see it that way at all. Nothing concrete had been established about driver seniority except for a loose arrangement that whoever had established a lead on points early in the season would be regarded as Number One and therefore be backed up by the other driver. The race at Jarama looked like being a big chance for Mass if he played his cards right.

The Grand Prix of Spain marked the return of the 'circus' to Europe for another year. The event coincided with the announcement of a revised set of measurement regulations aimed at keeping cars within accepted limits and simplifying the control of the technical regulations. The Formula 1 Constructors' Association had welcomed the implementation of the new regulations, and in fact had helped to draw them up. To avoid making current cars obsolete on May 1, the day before the Spanish Grand Prix, the maximum size measurements had been drawn up around existing cars so that

Right: Hunt's first race for the Marlboro-McLaren team was in the Brazilian Grand Prix. His M23 looks curiously dated with an airbox high over its engine

Following pages: this superb study gives an impression of the strains that can be imposed on a Grand Prix car, and perhaps just an inkling of the knife edge the driver is riding

Left, top: season-
long rivals – Niki
Lauda leading Hunt
in the opening laps
of the Spanish
Grand Prix
Lower: worry
session at Zolder –
Hunt, Mayer and
Caldwell ponder
over the M23
handling malaise
before the Belgian
Grand Prix

the widest car – a McLaren M23 – was measured, and its width was
regarded as the maximum. Likewise the longest car was measured,
and its length was written in as the maximum for all cars. It made
sense then.

Two other circumstances were to make the Spanish Grand Prix
unusual. Between the Long Beach and Jarama meetings Niki Lauda
came close to killing himself when he fell from a tractor while moving
earth on the site of his new home in Austria. The tractor tipped with
a load of earth high in the scoop, and Lauda somehow fell down
between the seat and the transmission as the tractor rolled. He
struggled out with earth caked in his eyes and mouth, shaken and in
pain from broken ribs. There was a strong chance that he would be
unable to defend his title lead in Spain, but the doctors were under-
estimating Lauda's cast-iron will. He reported for duty in Spain
after being given a pain-killing injection. Now he said his only problem was that he could feel the jagged rib ends grinding together
under the G-forces in hard cornering.

The Spanish race was also to see the debut of the new six-wheeled
Tyrrell driven by Patrick Depailler, and other teams were watching
to see if the new concept would match the predictions of its designer,
Derek Gardner.

Thus it was to be no ordinary race, though the grid looked familiar
with Hunt on pole position, three-tenths of a second faster than
Lauda in the Ferrari beside him. Behind Hunt was Depailler in the
six-wheeler, and beside him was Mass in the other Marlboro-
McLaren. Three-tenths of a second gained in practice by a driver
sound in wind and limb had to show up in the race as an advantage
over a driver soldiering on with broken ribs round the tight loops
and twists of the two-and-a-tenth mile circuit. But again Hunt was
beaten from the line out of respect for his transmission and lost
ground because of it. His ability to outpace the field in practice only
to dump that advantage at the start compares with the golfer who
slams on to the green in two every time and then four-putts. When
the race had settled down after the usual cut and thrust of the
opening laps, Lauda was leading with Hunt as his shadow, a gap to
Depailler with the six-wheeler, and then Mass. Hunt was content
to play a waiting game, knowing that Lauda's ribs wouldn't let him
call the pace for the entire race.

*I followed him when he was motoring hard at the start and I was able to tuck
in their quite comfortably. I couldn't do anything about passing him, it was
just a case of waiting until his ribs started to hurt and I'd be able to nip
through.*

On lap 32, just before half distance, Hunt took the lead, Mass
following him into second place a couple of laps later. Depailler's
race had ended a few laps earlier with brake failure, when his six-
wheeler had skittered backwards into the catch-fencing.

*Niki cooled it as soon as I went through and it was quite obvious that he
wasn't going to give chase, so there was no point in busting a gut or the car at
that point. Jochen pulled up to me and was then instructed to hold position.
I knew he wouldn't pass me because I'd seen his pits signal board telling*

him to stay there, but he was running so close behind me that if I missed a gear he couldn't help but pass me at that range. If he went by then, I could understand him being very reluctant to let me through to the lead again because of our tenuous team situation. Let's face it, Jochen was driving very well in Spain and if he'd been from another team and was racing me, I doubt that I could have got away from him without a battle.

Ten laps from the finish, Mass dropped out of Hunt's mirrors in a plume of oil smoke as his engine blew up on the sweep down from the right-hander before the pits, and Hunt cruised on to victory. After the race, Hunt had words with Mayer about their team tactics, asking him to tell Jochen not to stay right on his exhaust pipes. It was a problem that did not arise again until the final race in Japan, when Mass again moved into second place and drove just beyond the spray of Hunt's rear wheels until the German driver misjudged one of the rivulets left after the rain had stopped and skated off the road.

Hunt's Spanish victory, 30·97 seconds clear of Niki Lauda, was popular, but as it turned out Hunt had to wait weeks before his win

Mass following Hunt at Jarama

This car is too wide! Hunt's M23 in the Spanish Grand Prix

was confirmed. He was taken through all the motions of winning, the presentation by the King of Spain, the jubilation within the team for their first championship victory of the season . . . then the win was taken away when official scrutineering revealed that his M23 was too wide across the rear wheels. Hunt was relaxing in the Marlboro motorhome.

We felt that we had earned a win by this stage. We had won two non-championship races but until then luck had been working for us on the wrong days. Then they told us we had been disqualified. First of all they told us there had been a problem about the width of the car and the stewards were meeting to decide what to do. There was no point in getting uptight about it. There was nothing we could do if the car was too wide.

It was after eight o'clock and getting dark before the sentence was handed out by the stewards, and a journalist brought the word to Hunt that his win had been taken away. Recalling the scene now, Hunt says his reaction was: *Well, fine. It's a bit of a bore. What's going to be done about it?* At the time he looked grey, numbed by the news, as though he wasn't taking in the fact that his eagerly anticipated first win for McLaren had been snatched away. Perhaps subsequent disappointments and defeats during the summer have made the first one seem less significant to him than it really was at the time.

The technical committee of the sport's governing body, the Commission Sportive Internationale (CSI), had been asked to make a showing at the Grand Prix at the express wish of the Formula 1 Constructors' Association so that the CSI men could be seen to be doing a job of policing their new regulations instead of acting like exiled kings, governing from afar, collecting the taxes, but really doing little. The measurement and repeat measurement across the back of Hunt's winning car kept registering the same fact: that it was too wide, by only 1·8 centimetres – say five-eighths of an inch – but too wide nevertheless. Having been dragged along to do something, to show that the CSI still had teeth, they disqualified the winner.

Teddy Mayer brought his American legal training swiftly into action and early on Monday morning he was in Madrid arranging to file an official protest against the decision which gave the Grand Prix victory to second place man Niki Lauda. Mayer was not disputing that his car was too wide, even if the discrepancy was only the bulge in the Goodyear tyres. He was protesting against the severity of the sentence, saying it was like being hanged for a parking offence and that since the minute oversight could have given no possible advantage to Hunt, he should at least be able to keep his driver's points.

When Mayer's appeal was upheld later in the summer, Hunt's victory was restored along with the championship points and prize money, and the team was fined three thousand dollars. The winner's purse must have been close to fifteen thousand dollars, from which they could handsomely afford to pay the fine. It made a ridiculous situation even more ridiculous.

The Points Famine
Belgium, Monaco
and Sweden

Team manager Mayer had argued with some conviction in Spain that the extra five-eighths of an inch could not possibly have helped his driver to win the Grand Prix at Jarama. Yet the fact remained that for the next three races, with the rear track narrowed to comply with regulations, James Hunt simply dropped out of the front line.

He had started the season confident that with the McLaren he could compete on equal terms with world champion Lauda, which in turn meant that Hunt thought himself equal to the task of taking the title. But with four rounds gone in the 16-race championship his task looked hopeless. He had won one race and finished second in another, but his disqualification in Spain left him with only the six points from his second place to Lauda in South Africa. The vital fractions of an inch in Spain had presented Lauda with a win he did not expect and had bumped his total up to 33 points. Hunt was fifth in the standings, still one point behind Mass since neither had scored points in Spain. If Hunt was still ambitious enough to be thinking about the world title he would also have worked out that he needed three Grand Prix wins just to draw level with Lauda, always supposing that Lauda scored no points at all in these three races. The Austrian, it appeared, could effectively take six weeks holiday.

The disqualification had suddenly made all teams aware that it could easily happen to them, since it was transparently obvious that it was a mistake on the part of the McLaren team. Being publicly thrown out of the race in Spain really hurt Mayer, who prides himself on meticulous attention to detail. From now on they would go over the cars with a micrometer and vernier calipers to make sure they were absolutely legal.

Another of the new rulings that came into force in Spain set down specifications for mounting oil containers on the car. Because the engine is tucked in behind the driver, cooling is a problem. Water radiators are mounted along the rear sides of the M23, and until the Spanish Grand Prix the small oil coolers had been fitted below the rear wing aft of the transmission. The new regulations called for the wing to be moved forward slightly, so the oil radiators were shifted to a new position just inside the water radiators on the right-hand side of the car. The McLaren men worried that their re-positioned oil coolers might somehow contravene the regulations and after the fracas in Spain, they could not afford to take chances. In fact Mayer convinced the CSI men that there was a difference in definition between oil containers (oil tanks) and oil coolers which circulate oil to cool it, and although he won his point a doubt remained. The team planned to return the oil coolers to their old position before the next race.

This was the Grand Prix of Belgium on the 2·6-mile Zolder track, not a favourite with the drivers because it is tight, featureless and artificial, with few areas in which to pass. It encouraged follow-my-leader racing rather than offering a real challenge to a Grand Prix star. The traditional home of the Belgian Grand Prix had been the classic road course at Spa-Francorchamps, a super-fast countryside circuit, but damned by freak weather. Thunderstorms could loom in minutes, deluging one part of the track while the remainder stayed dry. This had happened during the Grand Prix in 1966, triggering a series of multiple accidents as the cars skated out of control on dry tyres. So the once-proud Belgian Grand Prix had been relegated to Zolder, a circuit previously used only for lesser events.

On the first day of practice Hunt's name was at the top of the timing sheet ahead of Regazzoni's Ferrari and of Scheckter, who was having his first drive in the second six-wheeler car. Between that first morning practice and the afternoon session Hunt's mechanics set about shifting the oil coolers back to their old position below the rear wing. The modification had been scheduled to be carried out at the factory between the Spanish and Belgian races, but time had run short.

We put them back virtually where they had been under the wing, but because the wing had been moved forward, the coolers were now about an inch away from their old position. No more than an inch . . .

Hunt and Scheckter running neck and neck down to a left-hander at Zolder, Chris Amon following in the Ensign

The effect was to be remarkable; Hunt's car turned 'evil' and it took more than a month to pinpoint the problem. In the second session he was ninth fastest, and in the final timed run he was eleventh fastest. He started in the race on the second row of the grid by virtue

of his time in the first session. He tagged on in second place behind
Lauda from the start but his car was impossible, the McLaren not
handling consistently. Lauda started piling up a lead while Hunt,
rather than heading the cars behind, was holding them up.
Gradually car after car passed him: Regazzoni in the second Ferrari,
Laffite in the Ligier-Matra, Depailler and then Scheckter in the
other six-wheeler. Hunt found it hard to believe – and there seemed
nothing he could do to stop them. Added to his handling problems,
Hunt's car was now smoking badly, and at half distance it finally
ground to a halt with a seized transmission. Lauda went on to win
from Regazzoni, the Ferraris 1–2 across the line. Laffite was third
in the Ligier, and Scheckter fourth.

Lauda was striding away with the championship, paying scant
heed to the broken ribs that were still paining him enough to need
electroshock treatment. He had a total of 42 points, ahead of
Regazzoni now with 15 and Depailler with 10. James Hunt was
seventh in the standings, still with six points, and his team-mate
Mass, sixth at Zolder, was fourth in the standings with eight points.

The scene now moved to Monte Carlo, where James Hunt was
not going to give the thousands of British enthusiasts anything to
cheer about. The M23 that had been so fast in the early-season
races was now a pig to drive, and for no good reason that anyone
could identify. Hunt qualified on the seventh row of the grid, Mass
on the sixth. On race morning, for the warm-up session they tried
taking the airbox off the top of the engine and found that this improved the performance of the rear wing by tidying up the airflow.

Trying it for size?
climbing into
Lauda's 312T at
Zolder, while its
'owner' looks mildly
apprehensive and
the Ferrari
mechanics find it all
highly amusing

First-lap scramble through the Station hairpin at Monaco, Mass on the inside, Pace, Amon and Nilsson following

The car was not quite good but on full tanks it was handling well. The dreadful problem was that I was so far back on the grid I wouldn't be able to pass anybody simply because there isn't anywhere to pass at Monaco without doing anything risky or stupid. We know the form when we go to Monte Carlo. We know that the race is decided on your grid positions, so we know that practice is super important. Because you're on the pole doesn't necessarily mean you're going to win, but if you're on the pole and you don't break down, you've done a pretty feeble job if you don't finish in the first three. I suppose it's all right to go to Monaco and do that once a year but it's a pretty stupid way to have a race.

When the race started Hunt had to join in the queue from twelfth position though he had the pace to be with the leaders.

I was running two seconds a lap slower than I wanted to simply because there was nowhere to pass, and I have to say that I spun the car through my lack of interest, sheer bloody frustration. That dropped me to the back of the field, and when I was lapping on my own I was as fast as Niki who was leading. Then I caught the bunch battling for last place and I could make no impression on them at all. Immediately I was lapping three seconds slower than I had been.

On the 24th lap, the engine blew up – that form of mechanical failure in racing language covering anything from a dropped valve to a broken crankshaft, a small breakage to a failure that could literally cut the motor in half – and Hunt was frankly grateful for the release. *Looking back, we were very fortunate to have our blow-ups and breakdowns at times when it didn't matter. It could have been very expensive for us if I'd had the Monaco engine blow-up when I'd been leading. You have to expect breakdowns during a season, and any team that doesn't have at least one engine failure in a race during the season has frankly just been lucky. You can prepare the engines just so well, but you can never guarantee them . . . So it's important to have your problems at the right time. The gearbox seized in Belgium when it didn't matter, and the engine blow-up at Monaco was the only motor problem we had all season in any race, other than the drama in*

Brazil with the fuel injection trumpet falling off and jamming things.

Niki Lauda won as he pleased, and was followed across the line by the Elf-Tyrrell six-wheelers of Scheckter and Depailler. Lauda's score was now 51 points. Hunt was still pegged on the board at 6, and Mass had finished fifth in Monaco to move up to 10 points. Hunt's challenge for the championship was fading into insignificance.

In Sweden for the seventh Grand Prix at Anderstorp, Hunt was 14th in the first practice session, 11th in the second session and 8th in the final session for a grid position on the fourth row.

After the first day of practice in Sweden we were really tearing our hair out and we decided in desperation to put the car back exactly to Spanish settings. One thing we knew for sure was that it had nothing to do with the car being five-eighths of an inch too wide. Everyone else wasn't sure, but we knew it was absolutely nothing to do with that. The McLaren was set up exactly as it had run in the Spanish Grand Prix with the exception of the oil coolers which had to stay at the back under the wing because they didn't have the equipment to make the change in Sweden. It made no difference to the car, no difference at all. It was still 'evil'.

Jody Scheckter qualified his six-wheeler on pole position with Mario Andretti alongside him on the front row with the John Player Lotus. Was the two-and-a-half mile Swedish track really a Tyrrell circuit? In 1974 Scheckter and Depailler had finished first and second in their four-wheeled 007 Tyrrells and Depailler had set up a lap record that still stood. Andretti stormed off into a healthy lead from the start but was penalized a minute for jumping the gun, which meant that while he was leading on the road in fact Scheckter was leading the race from second place. On the 45th lap Andretti's engine blew up, and Scheckter and Depailler slipped into first and second slots for a repeat of their 1974 1–2 domination. Lauda was third, and Hunt was fifth.

The season was now moving to the halfway point, with the French

Hunt applying left lock to check a slide in his oversteering M23 at the exit from a left-hand corner at Anderstorp. For the next race the car's handling was to be transformed as the oil radiators were moved to the side, where a Texaco decal appears ahead of the rear wheel in this shot

Race winner in
Sweden was Jody
Scheckter in a
Tyrrell – the best
showing for one of
Ken's six-wheelers
in 1976

Grand Prix on the Paul Ricard track between Marseilles and Toulon
as the eighth race in the 16-race championship. There would have
been no takers for bets that Lauda was not going to repeat his world
championship win. The six-wheelers had beaten him in Sweden
but then Sweden was dubbed a freak track where freak things happened, never to be repeated during the rest of the season; as a
pointer to form Sweden could be ignored.

By this time the McLaren team was nearing panic. They had set
the car back to the Spanish Grand Prix configuration apart from
remounting the oil coolers.

*We were pretty sure that the mounting of the oil coolers wasn't the problem.
There was nothing to suggest that it could be, no physical, apparent reason.
Sure, we knew that oil radiators at the back could affect the rear wing but they
had been moved only so minutely from their old position relative to the wing,
that we couldn't believe it would be that.*

As there now seemed to be no alternative, the oil coolers were re-
mounted at the side of the car and the team went down to the Paul
Ricard track to test before the Grand Prix. Within a handful of laps,
Hunt knew they had pinpointed the problem. It was a different
car, different in the sort of way that made it feel like a front row car
and a race winner again.

Changing the position of the oil coolers by less than an inch under
the rear wing had been enough to upset the extremely sensitive
pressure area and spoil the airflow. It was a vivid reminder to the
team and to Hunt that the aerodynamic balance of the car, the
important compromise between air lift and downwards pressure
worked out in fractions of a degree, could make the difference between winning and losing. Hunt now looked at the championship
score with a less jaundiced view than he had been taking over the
past six weeks. He was a massive 47 points adrift on Lauda and
surely didn't consider himself still in contention for the title, but he
was going to fight for it.

The Turning Point
Victory in France

The McLaren team knew that their jinx had been licked by switching the positions of the oil coolers, but as the teams prepared for the Grand Prix in France this was still private knowledge.

Robert Langford, secretary of the Grand Prix Drivers' Association in its affiliation with the Constructors' group, and also a Wimbledon tennis umpire in his spare time, voiced the thoughts of a growing number of people: 'It really is quite embarrassing, you know. I visit friends who know absolutely nothing about racing and I have to

Calm and confident – Hunt and Mayer during practice for the French Grand Prix. Communications system plugs into driver's helmet, makes conversation possible without removing the helmet or shouting above other pits lane noises

Strain of driving hard shows in Hunt's face as he is interviewed at the Paul Ricard circuit after the French GP

explain all the dramas. I told them that James had been disqualified from the Spanish Grand Prix on a technical infringement and that the five-eighths of an inch could not possibly have made any difference to the performance of the car. But now they are asking me what has been happening to James . . . that if the extra width made no difference, why is it that he hasn't been in the results since then? It's quite difficult to explain.' But the old spirit was back in the McLaren team at the Paul Ricard track: there were jokes in the pits; confidence had returned.

The Grand Prix of France alternates between circuits, but in 1976 the race was held on the 3·6-mile track set back in the hills behind the coastal resort of Bandol near Le Castellet for the second time in succession because of political wrangling at other tracks. The track had been financed by the drinks magnate Paul Ricard and it bore

Latin temperament shows as Ferrari designer Mauro Forghieri makes a point to his number one driver, Niki Lauda

his name. Most of the teams stayed in Bandol enjoying the local atmosphere, the sea-front restaurants and bars. Hunt was at the Ile Rousse Hotel, set back from the seafront but backing down to a sandy, sheltered little beach where more and more topless bathers appear each year.

In the first practice session Hunt was second fastest to the 12-cylinder Brabham-Alfa Romeo driven by Carlos Pace, and in the second session was fastest, just ahead of Lauda's Ferrari. The times stood through the final session to produce the front row of the grid, with Hunt on pole position.

For the race the team had decided to take a gamble on the tyres on Hunt's car. In practice they had realized that the Goodyears were changing their characteristics with wear.

They were soft compound tyres and they were tending to run hot, especially when they were new, but once they settled in they were a lot quicker and a lot more consistent in their behaviour. They didn't launch the car into a big understeer or a big oversteer.*

Oversteer is the quick way, but it's difficult to drive. It's fast, if you can cope with it. When I'm trying to pull out a quick lap at the end of practice I'll set the car up with as much oversteer as I can cope with. Understeer is the slow way round.

Hunt's Goodyear gamble was based on starting the race with a set of part-worn tyres which he knew – or hoped – would stay the same throughout the race without changing their characteristics. Lauda was starting with a new set of tyres, scrubbed a little by a few laps in the morning warm up. He made the best of the start, but Hunt hoped his tyre tactics would give him the measure of the Ferrari driver.

Niki set off at a great rate of knots and started to pull away, but I wasn't unduly concerned except for the fact that I was having to cope with oil or water blowing out the back of the Ferrari, indicating he would soon have a major problem with his car. The liquid wasn't troubling Niki because there would be 25 cars over it before he completed a lap and arrived back on it, but I was first to hit whatever it was and I was sliding all over the place.

Then it all turned sour for Ferrari. Although Lauda had pulled away in those opening laps, Hunt had started to eat into his rate of increase. The gap was steadying. On the eighth lap Lauda's engine blew up on the back straight and he coasted to a halt with the crankshaft broken. Eleven laps later Regazzoni's Ferrari suffered a similar engine failure and hurled him backwards into the catch fencing. Hunt was now leading comfortably from Depailler in the Elf-Tyrrell six-wheeler. He held onto the gap for a little while and then it gradually started to grow. *In the second half of the race I was able to ease off because he was dropping back then. I could open the gap by this time without going flat out.*

It was fortunate that Hunt had been able to build this 'cushion'

*Understeer is a handling condition where the car 'pushes' in corners, wanting to plough straight ahead instead of going round the corner. Oversteer is when the tail of the car wants to come out, and the car tries to spin.

Anxious period as
the French
scrutineers examine
Hunt's M23. Alastair
Caldwell and Tyler
Alexander (on one
of his rare excursions
to Europe from
McLaren's American
base) hold the rear
wing, by the left
rear wheel Teddy
Mayer waits for the
verdict, in the group
on the left Ken
Tyrrell jokes with
Peter Warr of Lotus.

of a few seconds to the little Frenchman because as they raced into
the final quarter of the Grand Prix Hunt began to feel ill. He had
been bothered by a stomach upset after dinner on the Friday night,
and now he was nauseated inside his helmet and mask, dry heaving,
fighting back the urge to vomit. Then the chequered flag was out
and Hunt was more relieved than usual to see it. Depailler was $12\frac{1}{2}$
seconds behind in second place, John Watson appeared to be third
and Carlos Pace fourth. At the scrutineering after the race there
was pandemonium as the French officials delved into their rule
books and began measuring the cars. Each of the top finishers was
minutely examined and the decision was taken to exclude third-
place finisher Watson from the results because the rear wing of his
Penske car was found to be $1\frac{1}{2}$ centimetres too high.

There was a long celebratory dinner at the hotel that night. At
crack of dawn the next morning Hunt and Mayer were to meet
Lotus chief Colin Chapman, who was flying them to Paris in his
company plane. Chapman was testifying on their behalf in the

McLaren appeal against the severity of the sentence in the Spanish Grand Prix disqualification.

We presented the case in Paris and they agreed with us that the punishment didn't fit the crime. We asked for a suitable fine instead of disqualification and that's what we got.

Hunt's Spanish victory and his championship points were reinstated and as a reprimand the team was fined $3000. Suddenly Hunt was reeling under a windfall of points. He had effectively moved 21 points closer to Lauda in two days. On Sunday at the Ricard track he had won nine points, and on Monday in Paris he not only regained his nine Spanish points but Lauda was docked three points when his position in Spain was dropped from first to second. Lauda now had 52 points and Hunt was up to 26, half the champion's points score at the halfway point in the season.

The reversal of the decision by the stewards in Spain was not at all well received in Italy and Enzo Ferrari called it 'a wicked verdict – we did not protest, but the McLaren car was breaking the rules before the race, and after the race.' His view was that Hunt's car had been illegal in Spain because it was too wide, and that even the McLaren team were admitting their car was illegal. How, then, could they win an appeal against disqualification? The saving grace at this point in the year was the fact that Lauda looked capable of staying in control of the championship from his commanding points position. The three poor races by Hunt had surely taken the steam out of the British team's challenge.

The championship still didn't look at all good for me, but at that point I had the attitude that I would have basically for the rest of the season. I was keeping an eye on the championship, for sure, but I had to take every race as it came and just try to win it because whatever happened to Niki and the Ferrari was not really relevant to me at that point. There was nothing I could do about it. I'd run my race, try to win it and when I got out of the car at the end of the race I'd look at the results and see how I was getting on in the championship.

At that stage it looked as though the championship was between Niki and Niki. Or between Niki and the Gods. We were starting to get results again but we weren't 'hot'. I felt that we had the potential if we got lucky as well. You need a bit of good luck, let's face it, and so far we'd had a lot of bad luck. Looking back on the season now they would just about cancel each other out. You don't get a string of results like we had in the second half of the season without good luck. But you make your luck in the long run.

Looking back on Hunt's three 'lost' races in mid-season, designer Gordon Coppuck feels that it wasn't so much the difference the placing of the oil coolers made to the car, as the difference those fractions of a second made to Hunt's position on the grid. 'Let's face it, if we had been in tenth place on the grid and suddenly dropped down to 14th or 15th, nobody would have noticed. But in our case we had the spotlight on us and it was recognizable. In fact the difference in placement of the oil coolers was a fairly intangible thing, but it's a mark of how super competitive Formula 1 has become. You can't afford to risk even fractions of seconds without it showing on your grid position.'

Trouble Starts
The British Grand Prix

In Britain Hunt had become a cult figure, a Mick Jagger personality, loved or hated with equal vigour. Hunt tends to encourage both attitudes by his way of life – casually exciting, outrageously successful – and it must be easy to dislike someone who makes success look so simple. Yet James Hunt is British and proud of it. Racing the Hesketh with the Union Jack as its only decal had somehow suited him, and more than anything else he wanted to win the British Grand Prix. In 1976 his fans knew he had a good chance at Brands Hatch.

Both sides of Hunt were brought out in public during the two weeks before that British Grand Prix. He had been entered in the Texaco Tour of Britain with BBC radio disc jockey Noel Edmonds, himself an enthusiastic saloon car racer. The pair were to share a Vauxhall. There was a problem over tyres that altered the handling of the car and indirectly led to Hunt slamming into a tree on a special stage, a timed section over a closed stretch of forestry road, early in the event. Both men were public personalities and their discussion – amicable and reasoned, according to Hunt – was blown across the front pages as a quarrel, with Hunt apparently behaving like a spoilt child when Edmonds wanted to have the car repaired and continue in the rally. Hunt wanted to quit. There was another incident later in the event when they were stopped by the police for speeding while trying to make up their lost ground, and this also reached the headlines. Whatever his views, and whatever the extenuating circumstances, as in the Long Beach incident with Depailler, Hunt emerged badly.

I won't say I behaved very well on the Tour, but the outcome was a combination of circumstances and sensationalist reporting. The combination of circumstances was the fact that several separate small incidents happened; taking them into a combination made them quite big, and then exaggerating each story individually made the whole thing very big. That's really what happened. They said that Noel Edmonds and I had a row, which is complete and utter rubbish. We never had a cross word of any sort. We discussed the pros and cons and I thought we should stop. Noel thought we should go on. It was blown up out of all proportion. It was one of those days when it would have been much better if I'd stayed in bed . . .

A few days later, there was wild applause in the Albert Hall after Hunt's trumpet solo during a special televised Grand Prix 'Night of the Stars'. His trumpet performance might be compared to the dancing bear – applauded not so much concerning the quality of the dance as the fact that it could do it. Hunt was back on top,

Britain's blue-eyed boy again instead of the spoiled brat who had been cutting up rough with the housewives' favourite disc jockey.

Brands Hatch drew a capacity crowd to see the battle between Hunt and Lauda. It was years since a Grand Prix crowd in Britain had been so charged with enthusiasm, so eager to see a British driver with a chance of winning on home ground. Jackie Stewart had been able to do just that but somehow it was more difficult for enthusiasts to identify with the brilliant little Scot. Hunt was different, he wore jeans and he drank beer: the crowd could identify with that.

If Hunt was regarding the championship on a race-to-race basis, aiming at individual victories rather than keeping tabs on his title score, Lauda was every bit as anxious. He was comfortably ensconced at the top of the table, but he needed more wins for his own satisfaction, if only because winning maintained his reputation and damped down Hunt's.

Lauda was on pole position for the Grand Prix at Brands Hatch with Hunt to his right, six hundredths of a second slower on the 2·6-mile Kentish track. Pole position was normally on the right-hand side at Brands Hatch, for an inside run to the first corner, the terrifying drop-away right-hander at Paddock Bend. But the track at the start–finish line is slightly banked and it is possible to slide sideways towards the verge on the slope of the road as the wheels spin at the start. Lauda chose to start from the left, the higher side, to get a long angled run into Paddock Bend. Regazzoni's Ferrari was tucked in behind Hunt. Behind Lauda was Andretti's black John Player Lotus.

Motor cycle World Champion Barry Sheene and girl friend are interested spectators as Hunt forcibly discusses a minor problem with Caldwell in the Brands Hatch pits

Right: the McLarens returned to form in the French Grand Prix. **Top:** Hunt leading a string of cars at the Paul Ricard circuit. **Lower:** relaxing with Jochen Mass and a pair of admirers . . . **Following pages:** last-minute bustle around the two front-row cars on the British Grand Prix grid at Brands Hatch, Hunt's McLaren and Lauda's Ferrari

Left: after the
second start at
Brands Hatch Hunt
is sandwiched
between the Ferraris
driven by Lauda and
Regazzoni

*It was going to be a really super race and for 150 yards it was. Until Clay
Regazzoni collided with Niki at Paddock Bend. I'd made my usual lousy
start, Niki had made a reasonable one and Clay had made a super start – a
real stormer. He went up on the left of me, sliced back in front of my car and
dived at the inside of Niki from way too far back. It was quite ridiculous.
Niki was already turning into the corner and Clay dived in and hit him. I was
able to enjoy it for I suppose half a second, because it was wonderful, extremely funny, for me to see the two Ferrari drivers take each other off the road.
But it quickly became obvious that I was in it too. I got on the brakes because
there was no way through, and I was punted up the rear. Then all hell broke
loose. I was into Regazzoni's car which was sliding backwards, and my rear
wheel climbed over his. My car was in the air, flying, and then it crashed down
again on its wheels. I didn't have a chance to be frightened or to realize that
I could have been on my head. I was just heartbroken that I'd done 150 yards
of the Grand Prix I'd hoped to win. The moment I landed, it was all action
again. In that sort of situation you've got to keep the engine running, put it in
gear and drive it to see what's happened to the car. Rather like falling in a
running race – you pick yourself up, dust yourself down and while you're
running you check yourself to see if you've got any breaks, bruises or cuts.*

That Paddock Bend scene had been awesome. Spectators could
see the red Ferraris tangling, clouds of smoke from tortured tyres,
dust and scattering cars. For incredible fractions of time one car was
teetering sideways, the whole raw underside of the monocoque
clearly visible, half a ton of racing car primed with 40 gallons of high
octane fuel, poised on the edge of disaster. It was Hunt's McLaren.
*I set off again but it was immediately obvious that the steering was damaged
because the car wasn't steering properly. The front suspension was damaged
too and it was leaping about but still just driveable. I was motoring through
the Druids loop wondering what the hell would happen now, wondering if
anyone had been hurt in the mêlée, when suddenly I saw the 'race stopped'
flags, the crossed yellow and oil flags, and I gave a whoop of delight. I thought
all my birthdays had come at once. One second I was despairing of my luck
and now it was all on again. I turned into the back road to the pits but because
the car wasn't steering properly and there were people crowding all over the
place, I abandoned the car and ran down the pit road to tell the lads to come
and do something about it.*

*I thought my race car would have been too badly damaged to repair before
the restart – there would obviously be a restart – and I wanted them to switch
my race wheels and tyres on to the spare car. I didn't know we weren't allowed
to use the spare car, but the team did a very professional thing. They decided
to repair the race car as well as getting the spare car ready as they didn't
know exactly which car we would be able to run at the restart. In fact we took
the spare car to the grid and put it in position while all the arguments went on
about whether we could do it or not, and by the time all the arguments had
finished, the race car had been repaired and the lads brought it up on to the
front row.*

The obvious solution was to re-form everyone on the grid and
restart the race, which could scarcely have deemed to be started
if it had virtually ended at the first corner, an unheard-of occurrence
in Grand Prix racing. It has been said that the dash from the starting

94

Chaos at Paddock Bend

Regazzoni (car No. 2) was over-ambitious as he tried to take advantage of Lauda's wide line into the corner, clashes wheels with his team leader; Hunt (behind the Ferraris) fleetingly enjoys the moment, Andretti (No. 5) looks for a way though.

Lauda has everything pointing the right way again, Regazzoni's Ferrari and Andretti's JPS are nose to nose, Hunt is trying to squeeze round on the outside, with Amon (No. 22) following him and Depailler (No. 4) steering into the clear space. Given another inch or two, Hunt would have got clear, but a rear wheel touched the Ferrari and flung the McLaren high into the air. Amon is still hard on his brakes, Laffite (No. 26) is confronted with a problem, and willy-nilly is heading for the bank in his Ligier.

After touch down, Hunt drives gingerly on, the front wheels of his M23 pointing in slightly different directions. Mass follows, and Pace (No. 8) looks for a way round Regazzoni's steam-shrouded Ferrari. Hunt watches the tail enders through . . .

. . . and Regazzoni is left amongst the dust and debris

grid to the first corner is the most dangerous period in any motor race as two queues of high-powered cars scramble for places in a single-file run through that first corner. In the chaos of flying cars, clouds of dust and earth, the senior Safety Observer at the corner had had to make an instant decision. He had erred on the side of caution, deciding that if he could not accurately ascertain the extent of the accident he should not allow the race leaders to plough into what could have been a disaster area. He called for the race to be stopped, yet only 60 seconds later it seemed that he had over-reacted because the track was clear enough for racing. But in the instant of decision he had been right. It was easier to withstand the wrath of the drivers who had been lucky and scraped through un-scathed on that first corner, than to have stood guilty of turning a spectacular accident into a holocaust. As the arguments on the rights and wrongs of the whole Brands Hatch issue gathered heat, it was alleged that perhaps the steward had deliberately ordered the race stopped to give Hunt a chance. Lauda had threaded his way out of trouble after the initial contact from Regazzoni which had slewed him sideways, and he was a clear leader when the race was red-flagged to a stop.

Hunt's McLaren, Regazzoni's Ferrari and Lafitte's Ligier-Matra had all been damaged in the accident and when the cars were called back to the grid, all three drivers appeared in their team's spare

His M23 restored to health, Hunt accelerates out onto the long circuit at Brands Hatch

Druids hairpin, lap 45. To the joy of the crowd Hunt has slipped past Lauda under braking and leads the British Grand Prix, in fact and on the road; the rule-makers much later decide otherwise . . .

cars. The huge crowd had their appetite for action whetted. There was a hush just like that around a *Plaza de Toros* as the new bulls are brought in. Then came the announcement that only those drivers who had completed the lap would be allowed to restart the race. It sparked an uproar from the crowd such as had never been heard from a British crowd at any motor race. From the football crowds on the terraces at Wembley, yes. From the enthusiasts at Brands Hatch, no. The heat of the crowd added to Hunt's determination. He would start the British Grand Prix, no matter what. He counted the crowd as his and he wanted to perform for them.

A startline official conveyed the message to him that he wouldn't be allowed to start in the spare car. He told the official that it was his race car repaired, unwilling to let regulations come between him and the start. He told his mechanics that nothing and nobody would prevent him from starting the race – even if they were to disqualify his efforts afterwards. Regazzoni, who had triggered the whole situation, was sitting on the grid behind Hunt's car, and the Ferrari management were saying that if James started in his spare car, why they would start Regazzoni in his. The argument now began to sway back and forth. Perhaps the first announcement had been a hasty one, perhaps the ruling was not quite as clear as it might have been, now they had looked at it again.

It seemed that if you were still running at the time the race was stopped, you could restart in your original car. But by now it was close to an hour since the accident and in the McLaren pit the

Best of friends –
Hunt and Lauda
after the British
Grand Prix

mechanics were putting the finishing touches to their repairs on
Hunt's car. A new steering arm and a front suspension link had been
fitted during the rebuild. The car was rolled up to the front of the
grid, pushed through the milling throngs of mechanics, journalists,
officials and hangers-on. Honour appeared to have been settled.
The grid was cleared and the crowd was ready for more action.

Lauda made the best of the second start, from Hunt and Regazzoni. Hunt was having his problems in left-handers because of the
way his car had been set up with 'stagger' in the rear tyres, a means
of adjusting the pressures to make one tyre very slightly larger than
the other, giving the car a right-hand bias to improve its handling
in the predominant number of right-hand corners at Brands Hatch.
*You juggle the pressures to play with the diameters of the rear tyres, running
a few pounds more in one tyre than the other, which is a pretty 'Black Art' sort
of thing to do and it takes a while for them to balance up. I had a lot of understeer in the left-handers to start with but I was quicker than Niki in the right-
handers. There are more right-hand corners than left on Brands Hatch, but
I was so nastily slow on the left-handers that I was making a gross loss to
Niki in the opening laps. You can't throw the car with full tanks because it
just won't throw – if it's pushing, it just pushes whatever you do because its
got all that weight of fuel forward.*

As the weight of the fuel load started to drop Hunt found that he
could 'throw' the car into the left-handers to create oversteer and
eliminate the understeer that was slowing him. At half distance in
the 76-lap race Lauda was still leading but Hunt was closing.
*I was really going well now, and about ten or fifteen laps before I actually
passed Niki, I knew I'd got him. I knew I was getting on top and our lap times
were coming down, down, down. It was quite fantastic. We were racing at*

Traditional
champagne shower
for the
photographers

*around 1 min 19 sec for a lap of Brands, the sort of times that Niki and I had
qualified at, flat-out with light fuel loads in practice!*

Hunt already held the Brands Hatch lap record at 1 min 23.78
sec (112.15 mph) but in their battle for pole position, Lauda had
turned in a lap at 1 min 19.35 sec. Hunt was only a fraction slower
at 1 min 19.41 sec. During the race the official lap record went to
Hunt again at 1 min 19.82 sec (117.71 mph).

*I'd been catching Lauda steadily but not enough and then I was helped by a
couple of back markers trailing the field. He got the worst of that, and about
five laps after that I started stabbing at him.*

It was on the 45th lap that Hunt finally drove up inside Lauda
on the climbing approach to the loop at Druids Hill. For the rest of
that lap the crowd was cheering and waving, ecstatic that their man
was in front.

*Then I was away and after about a lap he stopped fighting. That was nice but
I was on top and I wanted him to race me, not just hand over.*

Hunt was disappointed in Lauda that afternoon for not contesting the lead, and he wondered how seriously the gear linkage
trouble was hampering the Ferrari driver. Lauda said afterwards
that this had slowed him. Hunt was happy to have the win but he
felt robbed of the satisfaction of racing for it. It was like spending
three days gamefishing before you struck a marlin, only to have it
roll belly-up on the surface without a battle.

*But I don't know, maybe Niki was being more professional than me because
he knows if he can't beat you that way, then he'll drive to the finish. At
Brands Hatch he had miles on the next man, so there was no hurry and he
could re-adjust his pace. Personally I will always, even if I'm obviously
beaten, keep the pressure on to try to keep as close as I can and push him. I*

don't imagine I'd push him into a mistake because most of these guys won't make a mistake in those circumstances, but just in the unlikely event that he'll run out of petrol or have some other mechanical problem that wouldn't show if he wasn't under pressure. I will always, always, always fight and go as fast as I can to keep the other guy under pressure and that's the fundamental difference between us – Niki will leave it and drive for his finish.

I cruised around after that because if I'd kept my boot on the accelerator I would have lapped the field. Actually I was a bit annoyed with everybody else at Brands, because where were they? I needed Niki to get a whole lot less than six points for second place and in the normal way there would have been five cars in the 50 sec lead I had built up over him.

The protests were being lodged with the race stewards while Hunt was being presented with the trophies and laurels. As far as the crowd were concerned, honour had been satisfied; they were not to know about the political fight already brewing that would sour the rest of the season.

There were protests from Tyrrell, Copersucar and Ferrari. They protested that I wasn't running when the first part of the race was stopped. The enquiry was held in the control tower with evidence being given by the observers and marshals. They said their piece, and it was quite obvious that I had been running when the race was stopped, albeit slowly, and the stewards did what I thought to be a generous thing. They offered the other teams the opportunity to withdraw their protests, to save face and save their protest fee. Tyrrell and Copersucar withdrew because there was no cause to protest on the evidence supplied, but Ferrari kept their protest in because I don't think team manager Audetto had the authority to withdraw a protest once placed without permission from Ferrari.

The Ferrari protest was not withdrawn, and fermented a situation that was to become more heated and more politically motivated than anything in the history of Grand Prix racing.

That evening Hunt joined his friends in the car park for a barbecue. They had come down with tents and motorhomes for a party that would last until the car parks started to clear around midnight. Later Hunt would defend the rights of the crowd to see the motor race they had paid for without being diverted by the flim-flam of loosely written rules.

What the hell do they have a stupid rule like that for anyway? People pay to see a race so if there is an accident like that and the race is stopped – what happens if it's an accident like Silverstone?* If there are not enough spare cars to replace damaged machinery, then the people who didn't qualify for the original grid should be brought in . . . anyone who is there with a driving suit and a set of wheels should be out there to make up the field. Of course Regazzoni and Laffite should have been allowed to race in their spare cars.

The crowd at Brands Hatch were fantastic, they'd got fed up with the rules and they didn't want to hear any more rubbish. They wanted to see a motor race.

*The British Grand Prix at Silverstone was stopped after a 12-car pile-up in 1973 and restarted with all available undamaged cars. Generally speaking the number of cars allowed to start a race is calculated for safety, on the basis of a car per tenth of a mile of track. On the 2·65 mile Brands Hatch circuit 26 cars is the maximum allowed.

The German Grand Prix
and Lauda Crashes

The Nürburgring was never meant to be a safe track. The 14·2 miles of mountain park road were built in the late 1920s to provide work for the armies of unemployed, and drivers who went to the Nürburgring in those days, and for years afterwards, accepted it as a challenge. Later its twists and turns, climbs and swooping drops, and blind brows were cars leapt into the air became a compulsory nightmare for generations of racing drivers, striving to stay on the road and out of the trees. It was a yardstick: perform well at the Nürburgring and you were a man among men. When cars were front engined and racing tyres were narrow, the 'Ring really stretched resources of skill.

In recent years Scottish world champion Jackie Stewart led the crusade to reduce the fatal charm of the Nürburgring, and some of the traditional dangers were eliminated – blind brows were graded down to mild undulations, tree-shrouded corners were cleared. Parts of the track were made safer, but this also made the track quicker. The fastest lap in the first German Grand Prix on the Nürburgring in 1927 was 66·49 mph over the north and south circuits for a lap distance of 17·5 miles. In 1976 Jody Scheckter set the fastest lap in an Elf-Tyrrell six wheeler at 118·57 mph on the 'shorter' 14·2-mile circuit.

As the speeds rose the risk of an accident was maintained, and mistakes could still kill. Expensive safety measures gave the driver a better chance of survival should something go wrong, but drivers were still critical of the overall standard of safety at the 'Ring. Lauda was one of the bitterest opponents of racing on the Nürburgring. He said that if he made a mistake he deserved the consequences, but he did not feel that he should stand the risk of destroying himself if something failed on the car, something outside his control, and there was no room for a soft landing. To bring the safety standards of a track like Brands Hatch to the 'Ring, with marshalls who are trained experts every hundred yards, would require thousands of men and a training programme that would be unmanageable. Hunt considers that the easing of the Nürburgring's more daunting sections has perhaps turned the track into less of a yardstick than it was.

I think drivers in Formula 1 now are generally so good that they don't get floored by a difficult track, and you would be surprised how similar the form is everywhere. That's a tribute to the drivers.

But as Hunt studied the grid for the 1976 Grand Prix with his car in pole position, he was pleased because even in its emasculated form the 'Ring is the toughest track drivers race on in a season.

Niki and I are on the front row. Depailler third fastest, he's been up there all year, Stuck in the March fourth, showing his local knowledge as a German, Regazzoni fifth fastest on the third row with the Ferrari, Laffite well up, Scheckter, Pace . . . it's much as you would expect at any track during the season . . . Ronnie (Peterson) a bit further back but he had a troubled practice.

Whether they're frightened of the 'Ring or not, everybody wants to win there. Our main problem is that people think drivers don't want to race there but that's not true. What we say is that we don't want to drive there unless it is up to the safety specifications of every other track we race on. So we have the problem of making sure the track is safe, but we also have a political problem too because when we ask other tracks to do safety modifications for us they can say 'Look, you go and race on that bloody Nürburgring without those precautions – why should we bother?

I didn't particularly want to race under those circumstances but politically I felt it was the right thing to do because the drivers' safety committee did give the race organizers a three-year deal that included 1976. If we backed down on our deal, our credibility would have been seriously damaged at other circuits we have to deal with, which would have been a retrograde step and much more serious than just one more race at the 'Ring. When it comes right down to it, you either don't go, or you get on with the job of racing. The McLaren team got on with the job and I wound up on pole position again.

On race day morning it was threatening rain but as the starting time approached there was a suggestion that the clouds were lifting and the overcast would clear. As the cars roared off round the short circuit and came back behind the pits to rejoin the pit straight at the North Curve, only one of the 26 was fitted with dry-weather slick tyres. The fastest tyre in dry conditions is a tyre with no tread at all, a smooth slick which provides the car with enormous grip.

Hunt and Lauda together at the Nürburgring, during qualifying for the German Grand Prix. In deference to German requirements, the Marlboro embellishments have been removed from the McLaren . . .

Treaded tyres mean extra rubber and extra weight, but treads act as channels for water in wet conditions and decrease the risk of aquaplaning, when the tyre literally skis over the wet surface. But the treaded tyre is subject to heat build-up on a dry track so the drivers and team manager have to pay careful attention to the weather before a race. A dry-weather slick becomes uncontrollable in the wet, a wet-weather treaded tyre will wear out in the dry.

The driver making the gamble with slicks in the German Grand Prix was Hunt's team-mate Jochen Mass. Their in-team standings had been settled earlier in the season after Hunt's uncertainties in Spain, when he worried that Mass might be moving up to usurp the position he had assumed as number one driver in place of Fittipaldi, and Hunt was paying close attention to the German driver's tyre decision.

I wanted to go on 'dries' too, but with everyone else on 'wets' I wasn't going to be making too big a mistake. Some years ago in a Formula 2 race at the 'Ring the weather had been similar and I was in the middle of the grid on 'dry' tyres when everyone else was in 'wets'. When you're on the middle of the grid you're not going to win the race if you do the same as everyone else anyway, so I gambled on 'dries'. If it works, it works well and it certainly worked for Jochen in this Grand Prix. But in my Formula 2 race it rained and I came round miles last. In our current situation I reckoned that if we were all on the same tyres at the front of the grid, I could win the race anyway.

I hadn't bargained on Jochen's decision being quite as good as it was because he came through second only to Ronnie Peterson at the end of the first lap and soon passed him to take the lead. I stopped for dries on the first lap and so did a bunch of others including Niki.

As they completed the second lap and headed away on the third, Hunt had moved into second place some 45 seconds behind Mass, to put the McLarens first and second, with the German driver Mass leading on his home track and getting the same ego-surging lift that Hunt had been enjoying two weeks earlier in England.

After my pit stop I was apparently lapping fast enough to catch Jochen before the end of the race and there was already a panic in the pits because I needed a win! Alastair Caldwell was asking Teddy Mayer how they could stop Mass on his home track. It was a waste of time for the pit crew to hang out a signal 'LET JAMES WIN'. You just couldn't do it. My sympathies were entirely with Jochen. We'd had a pretty mediocre season up until then, here was his big moment, and he was really going well – in the same sort of situation I wouldn't have slowed down for anybody!

The decision was then abruptly taken out of the team's hands because as the two McLarens led the straggling race through the countryside the tail of the snake had stopped at Bergwerk with one car blazing and other cars parked as drivers fought to free its driver. Trailing cars were stopped because the track was blocked. The race was over. The burning car was Niki Lauda's Ferrari which had left the road, ploughed through the catch fencing and slammed into a bank, tearing the side out of itself and catching fire with the driver slumped in the cockpit. British driver Guy Edwards narrowly missed the Ferrari as it bounced back onto the track, but American Brett Lunger hit the wreckage in his Surtees and so did German driver Harald Ertl in his Hesketh. These three drivers were joined by a fourth, Italian Arturo Merzario, and in the absence of rescue marshals with proper equipment, the four of them waded into the flames in their fireproof driving suits and crash helmets.

I was well ahead of Niki on the road, maybe a mile ahead of him, so I knew nothing about the accident and drove 13 miles around the full lap until about two miles from where it happened before I saw the 'race stopped' flag signals were out. I eased up and there it was, with all the cars stopped. Niki had gone by this time and I chatted around with the other drivers to find out what had happened. Apparently Niki's car had been on fire, but he had got out of it and had talked to one or two of the drivers. He was burned a little bit around his face and wrists but it didn't look serious, and everything was fine. Niki was off to hospital, and obviously wouldn't be racing again that day but he'd have his burns patched up and we'd see him in Austria. That was the story we had then. It was still the story when we were getting ready for the re-start. There was suggestion now that he had a broken cheekbone from a smack on the face, and it was then out that his helmet had come off and that was how he had come to be burned. But there were no alarm stories and at the time it was evidently not serious at all.

The cars were taking their place on the grid for the second time that afternoon, and Hunt started the 'second part' of the Grand Prix in fairly good spirits because by that time it was dry and there was no uncertainty about tyres.

It was a good feeling to come round at the end of the first lap and see 'PLUS 10' hung out on the pit signal board when I went round the back of the pits, because it feels good to have ten seconds in hand on the first lap of the 'Ring. When I went off at the start I had put in a blinding first lap and the others were mucking each other about, spinning and falling about all over the place, which helped me, so I virtually had the race won by the end of the first lap unless someone was going to go immensely quickly after that. It was only a matter of controlling things from the front, which in fact was quite difficult because you've got to keep the pressure up at the 'Ring, because the lap is so long and you don't get the steady feed of information you get at other tracks. The point is that if you ease up at the 'Ring what was a 10 second lead could easily be only five seconds by the end of the lap and five seconds isn't a lot for another driver to pull back over 14 miles. So you've got to keep pressing on.

I felt sorry for Jochen, as well as for Niki, because in the first part of the race Jochen had really done everything he could out in the lead and it was a sort of testimony to his luck that the one time he really put it all together, fate intervened and ruined it for him.

Scheckter hauled himself into second place, but by the end of the race he was nearly half-a-minute back from Hunt as the winner, and Mass was right on his heels in the other McLaren in third place. It was the first time a McLaren car had won at the Nürburgring, and team manager Mayer, nicknamed 'The Wiener', a tag of unknown origin, was delighted.

My main memory of the 'Ring was the 'Wiener's' face, because McLarens had never won there and they'd always gone home with written-off cars in the truck. So when I stood on the winner's rostrum there was the 'Wiener' in his Goodyear cap, which doesn't fit him anyway – it's far too big for him – with that ridiculous grin on his face that he wears and can't wipe off. If you tell him to behave himself it just makes it worse, just splits him from ear to ear and he looks like a monkey standing there grinning. But it was tremendously gratifying to me. He's really an enthusiast, the 'Wiener', pure and simple. I mean he could do plenty of other things in life and make a lot more money but he goes racing because he loves it. To see that result was so gratifying for him . . . I got more pleasure out of that than I did from winning the race! He was absolutely thrilled, beside himself with joy after the race.

Mayer had arrived on the European racing scene as a punchy little lawyer from Scranton, Pennsylvania, to look after the driving career of his brother Tim, who was driving one of the works-supported Tyrrell Formula 3 Coopers in 1963. Tim was a potential champion, with a Cooper Formula 1 contract all but signed for the 1964 season, when the Mayer brothers joined forces with Bruce McLaren and his newly formed team to race a pair of $2\frac{1}{2}$-litre Coopers on the Tasman series in New Zealand and Australia. In practice for the final race in the series at Longford in Tasmania, Tim's Cooper became airborne over a tricky brow, slammed into a tree and he was killed. For weeks it seemed that Teddy's boundless enthusiasm for racing had died too, but when he tried to go back into law at home he realized that racing was really what he wanted to do. He returned to Britain, invested money in McLaren's team and helped to build it into one of the most successful teams in motor racing. When Bruce McLaren was killed in a testing accident with a CanAm sports car at Goodwood in June 1970, Mayer assumed control of the company and kept it together, with teams running in Formula 1 as well as in CanAm sports car racing and at Indianapolis in North America.

Austria
the Italians apply pressure

Niki Lauda was not as lightly injured as the drivers had first thought, although some had their suspicions. Carlos Reutemann, the swarthy Argentinian who would leave the Martini-Brabham team to join Ferrari before the end of the season, said as the grid was forming up again at the Nürburgring that he couldn't see how a man could sit as long as Lauda had in a fire like that, and not be very seriously hurt. His fears had foundation.

News of Niki started filtering through during the night of the German Grand Prix and the next morning. In the evening when we were back at the hotel, we had been telephoning around trying to find out which hospital he had been taken to.

The next morning we realized that he was in a very bad way indeed. We were very concerned but there was little or nothing one could do. I couldn't visit him, so I went home and sent him a telegram. I can't remember what it said but it was something provocative to annoy him and then it told him to fight, because I knew if he was annoyed and fighting, he would pull through. If he relaxed and gave in, he would probably die. You've got to stay conscious and physically fight it yourself, and I knew Niki would be aware of that. It was suddenly very important to me that Niki should live, in a way that I hadn't realized, and I felt awful because there was nothing I could do about it. There I was sitting at home and enjoying life even when I didn't particularly want to . . . when I wanted to go and help or do something and I couldn't. It was a strange time for me. But then he started to get better and I thought 'Take it easy. Slow down. Don't rush it'.

Lauda still led the championship from his hospital bed, but now Hunt had squeezed the gap down to 14 points, 58 to 44. The situation was plainly closing in on Ferrari. During the week after the accident, with Lauda still fighting for his life, Ferrari announced that they were withdrawing from Grand Prix racing until such time as the rule book and the regulations were put in order. Enzo Ferrari considered that he had been cheated of two Grands Prix – the Spanish and the British – which were to the distinct advantage of the McLaren team, and Lauda's accident could have only precipitated Ferrari's announcement. The news was taken with a pinch of salt in quarters where such Ferrari withdrawals had been seen and heard before, but the 'Old Man of Maranello' was known to be a shrewd manipulator of situations to suit his own ends, and only the gullible were lured into believing that he meant what he said.

Ferrari's withdrawal after the German Grand Prix was the spark to start a flaring campaign in Italy critical of the efforts of the Marlboro-McLaren team. Hunt was at the centre of the storm and he reacted very strongly against the Italian manoeuvres.

Ferrari were really freaking out. They withdrew from racing forever and then withdrew for a few weeks. They were issuing statements right, left and centre.

Hunt went to the Osterreichring in Austria for pre-race testing just after the German Grand Prix, and while he was sitting on the pit counter, waiting to go out again, one of the track organizers told him of an amazing telephone call he had just received from Italy. *It was someone beseeching them to be patriotic Austrians, to think of Niki and to cancel the Grand Prix! In the light of what happened a few days later, that first phone call on the quiet was interesting. It had been made discreetly to the organizers, who had directly told me as a matter of personal interest, and there was nothing more to be said on the subject. For sure the organizers were not going to spread the suggestion that their race might be cancelled. When I went back to Austria for the race the following week, Ferrari had gone public in their move to stop the race. It was the most incredible thing I've ever heard. Something like that is a really clandestine manoeuvre – and there they were pushing it in the press.*

Lauda's accident in Germany had cast a pall over the Grand Prix at the Osterreichring because he has a tremendously loyal following in his home country and the crowd gave him their full support. At the track stalls and shops lining the entrance road there were Lauda tee shirts and caps, Lauda decals and flags and badges. Meanwhile, in an intensive care ward, Lauda was battling back to life. As Reutemann had feared at the time, Lauda had suffered internal injuries from the fire. His lungs were scorched and he had burns on his face and his head where the crash helmet had been knocked askew, perhaps by a pole in the catch-fencing. The Grand Prix circus was confident that Lauda would make it, now that he had won that initial confrontation with death. At times like this, the Grand Prix world draws very close together. Men who had devoted their whole year to beating everyone else could be seen mingling, wondering how Lauda was making out, knowing he would pull through because he was so tough. They were pleased for him. The circus, or 'family' as it has been called, can and does steel itself to cope with death because death and danger is what turns motor racing from a sport into a spectacle. When Lauda started his fight back to life, the 'family' was with him all the way.

The Austrian Grand Prix organizers, however, would suffer at the gate. It was bad enough that Niki would not be racing, but Ferrari's sudden withdrawal had effectively turned off the flood of enthusiastic Italians who pour over the nearby border between Austria and Italy to support their home team. That Ferrari had withdrawn was bad news for the Austrian promoters; the campaign to cancel the race was something else again.

It had also become obvious that with the championship so close between Lauda and Hunt, cancellation of the Austrian Grand Prix would give Niki a bonus fortnight for recovery, and Hunt one race less in which to harvest points while his opponent was out of action.

Rain had washed out the practice sessions but before it rolled down off the hills behind the circuit, Hunt had turned in a time

Close racing in
Austria – Peterson
heading Nilsson,
Scheckter and
Hunt

Right, top:
typically, Hunt
raises both arms
high out of the
cockpit as he takes
the flag at the end
of the German
Grand Prix, and
(**lower**) waves to
the crowd after-
wards; runner-up
Jody Scheckter is
on his left, third-
placed driver
Jochen Mass on his
right
Following pages:
Hunt leads the
restarted German
Grand Prix through
the first bends of the
Nürburgring,
followed by
Regazzoni and the
two Tyrrells driven
by Scheckter and
Depailler

that gave him pole position with Ulsterman John Watson alongside
him in the Penske. A year earlier, Penske team driver Mark
Donohue had crashed on the morning of the race when a tyre punctured, and had died later in hospital. His place in the Penske team
had been taken over by John Watson, who had first been encouraged
to compete by his father, who had raced a 500 cc car after the Second
World War. Hunt was nearly one second faster than Watson, but
he was in no doubt that times would have been closer if the rain
hadn't damped the competition.

*We knew that Watson was quite capable of going as fast, it was just that
I'd got organized, had a new set of tyres fitted and gone quick before he had a
chance to build up. The weather was threatening so I made sure to get my
good time in there and then. I wasn't going to sit around and wait for it.*

The Osterreichring is one of the newer tracks, laid out on foot-
hill slopes in beautiful countryside, 60 miles from Graz, and within
view of the Styrian section of the Alps. It is a fast 3·67-mile circuit,
and in the race Hunt was to set a new lap record at 137·83 mph.

The start of the race was delayed as thunderclouds threatened a
downpour, but the danger passed and the cars took the grid. The
drivers were aware of the rain and they were told that the race would
be stopped if spray appeared on the tyres, which were dry-weather
slicks. From the start Hunt led from Watson, but into the first fast
corner Watson moved into the lead, and as the field swept down
the long slalom from the top of the hill, Ronnie Peterson had joined
the leaders in his March. For two laps Watson led, then Peterson,
then Scheckter, three and four cars fighting for the front as they
came down off the right-hander and out of the trees on to the pit
straight. It was the closest racing the pit lane had seen in years. For
a lap Scheckter led in the six-wheeler, but then a pattern emerged
with Watson, Peterson and Swedish driver Gunnar Nilsson in the

Hunt and Watson
during their classic
duel in the Dutch
Grand Prix at
Zandvoort

Lotus ahead of Scheckter and Hunt. It was apparent that all was not well with Hunt.

Early in the Dutch race Hunt heading Peterson, Watson and Regazzoni

We had played with the car after I had run my fast lap, and I wasn't all that happy with it. We had an understeer problem on full tanks again. I thought we had cured that before the race started but it was getting worse and I was having a real struggle to stay on the road. Jody had an enormous accident at the top of the hill beyond the pits in the 14th lap, when the front suspension broke on his car, and I went skating through all the mud and debris from that, but it was obvious that whatever was wrong with my car wasn't anything to do with debris from Jody's crash.

After the race the mechanics discovered that the left front wing had been hit from underneath and the angle of the nose tabs had been flattened. A rock or something had actually pierced the underside of the wing. Mud in the hole indicated that this had happened before Hunt ran through the debris of Scheckter's crash, but Hunt had no recollection of having hit anything or having been hit by anything in those hectic opening laps when the damage must have occurred. He finished fourth.

The race had been won by John Watson, the bearded Irishman, scoring his first victory for the Penske team on the track that had killed their driver a year before. Watson, elated at his first win, obeyed bets to shave off his beard and raced clean-chinned for the rest of the season.

Hunt was less than delighted with his fourth place that afternoon in Austria but one particular television viewer was sitting up in his hospital bed and getting an enormous amount of satisfaction from Hunt's modest placing. After all, Lauda was still the World Champion and Hunt's fourth place was worth only three points. As the scene switched to Zandvoort on the coast of Holland for the Dutch Grand Prix, the score was: Lauda 58, Hunt 47.

The Hunt
mental
file cards on
Ronnie
Peterson
John
Watson

Recently I have found Ronnie a bit of an enigma. Two or three years ago he was undoubtedly the quickest guy around in Formula 1. He has a super talent – probably more than anybody else in Grand Prix racing, and certainly greater than mine – and at the time when he was at his Formula 1 peak, in 1973 and 1974, he combined that natural talent with a lot of experience. He really seemed to be the best driver around. Perhaps it was not his fault that his career went into the doldrums, with cars that were uncompetitive or gave a lot of trouble.

John is one of the good drivers to race against. Fast, tough, always a competitor, a man to beat on his day. But one of his problems was that the Penske team didn't find the reliability that you need in Formula 1. The handicap extended not just to failing to finish the race, but also to breakdowns in practice which cost John practice time, and he often ended up lower down the grid than he should have been. It's a team business and until they had a cohesive unit they could not be a big threat. It was a problem of newness – we had it with Hesketh Racing and we had it licked by the time they packed up.

In 1977 John Watson joined the Martini-Brabham team, to drive the Alfa Romeo-engined Brabham BT45

Birthday Treat
Holland

James Hunt celebrated his 29th birthday on the 29th August, the Sunday of the Dutch Grand Prix at Zandvoort. The omens looked good. Niki Lauda was continuing his remarkable recovery, and Hunt had spoken with him several times on the telephone, chatting for three quarters of an hour after the race in Austria. Hunt was aware now of an emotional bond with Lauda as the Austrian fought back after his accident, a feeling that he had not been aware of before, and one that would be probably consumed in the flaring anger and recriminations when Hunt heard three weeks later that he had lost his British Grand Prix win to the Ferrari protest. Now a little window opened on Hunt's personality, revealing the inner sympathies of a driver outwardly determined to become champion of the world. If Hunt had been asked why he had maintained contact with Lauda during his recovery, he probably could not have found the right words. Perhaps it was the realization that Lauda was coming back from taking the ultimate risk, from the brush with death that haunts every driver and every driver's family. It was Hunt acknowledging 'there but for the grace of God . . .'

A year earlier at Zandvoort, Hunt had won his first Grand Prix driving the Hesketh, a masterful performance during which he was chased hard by Lauda, who was then on top and running for the title with the Ferrari. That race marked Hunt as a driver who could keep a cool head under pressure. He had won and became confident in his mind that he could handle a situation that had been completely new to him – leading and winning a Grand Prix under pressure. A year later in Holland, Hunt's situation was different: now he was expected to win.

The year before I had felt I was under pressure leading, but now I felt relaxed leading and under pressure if I was not. *That's a good way to feel because you're in command, in charge.*

Ronnie Peterson was getting back on form again by that stage in the season, the sort of form that had marked him as probably the fastest man in Grand Prix racing when Jackie Stewart retired at the end of 1973. Peterson was on pole position at Zandvoort in the March, eight hundredths of a second faster than Hunt's McLaren. Hunt spoiled his start again, letting Peterson away in the lead, and Watson was able to come through from the second row and take Hunt on the outside through the Tarzan Loop at the end of the pit straight. For the first seven laps the order was Peterson–Watson–Hunt, but Hunt was sitting there waiting to take advantage of the battle for the lead between Watson and Peterson. The Ulsterman

Hunt uses only one
arm to acknowledge
the flag at the end
of his second
winning drive in a
Dutch Grand Prix

was in flying form, buoyed with confidence after his Austrian victory, and was closing in on Peterson for the lead. They were duelling, and thus playing into the hands of Hunt, who was not really in a position to challenge seriously. His McLaren had started with understeer, and that became bad understeer as a brake air scoop came loose. Hunt took Watson on lap seven for second place and Peterson for the lead on the twelfth lap.

Actually I was taking advantages of their mistakes because I didn't really do any serious passing of anyone during the whole race. I nipped past Watson while he was still recovering from a big but unsuccessful go he'd had at Ronnie, and then when someone had blown up and dropped a lot of oil at one corner, Ronnie slid very wide and I simply drove quietly past him on the line. I didn't really overtake him at all. That put me in the lead, which was the best place to be because I had a real problem with the understeer, now aggravated by the fact that one of the fibreglass brake cooling ducts had broken away and was flapping around and interfering with one of the front wings. It meant that the onus was now on Watson to get past me – if he could. I think if he had got past me, he would have left me. When the brake duct broke away it really slowed me and John started to close in and have a go at the end of the straight each lap, nearly getting me but not quite. I wasn't weaving about off line or anything like that, but I was keeping a tight line down into the hairpin, forcing him to try the long way round the outside, but he never quite made it. Past the pits I was tucking in close to the wall because if I'd given him room there he would have been down the inside and gone.

On the 47th lap the Penske coasted to a halt at the end of the straight with bearing failure in the transmission. It was the last time during the season that Watson would be near the front. With some

30 laps to go, Hunt was now getting signals that Regazzoni, who had been driving a steady race, was now second in the lone Ferrari, the team having in fact stayed away for only one race despite their announcement of withdrawal from racing 'for ever'. It had occurred to Hunt that Regazzoni might have been entered in Holland for the same reason as had prompted Ferrari to try to bring about the cancellation of the Austrian race: to stop Hunt earning points.

I now had a big fight to the finish because although I was something like ten seconds ahead of Clay, I didn't want him to get within reach. Boy, was I in a panic!

Hunt won the race a scant car's length ahead of the Ferrari. The championship score now read: Lauda 58, Hunt 56. For the motor racing enthusiasts the tension was reaching fever pitch, while in the Ferrari and McLaren camps the atmosphere was electric.

After the race there was a giant birthday cake, baked and iced in the shape of the track at the behest of the race organizers, as a memento of Hunt's first Grand Prix win at Zandvoort the year before, and as a gesture for his birthday. James's mother was in the grandstands with his brother David. It was her first trip to a European race. She had been nervous as she waited for the Grand Prix to start, and even more nervous as she waited for it to end, but her anxiety gave way to relief and delight when she realized her son had won. She had also been to the non-championship races at Brands Hatch and Silverstone (both of which had been won by James) and Mr and Mrs Hunt had been invited to Monza for the Italian GP as guests of Marlboro. But the lucky streak her presence had produced was not enough to overcome the omens in Italy.

The Italian Confrontation

During the weeks leading up to the Italian Grand Prix at Monza in September, stories had been appearing in the Italian press to the effect that the McLaren team was running on illegal fuel, doctoring the regulation pump petrol with additives to improve performance. Methanol, an alcohol-based fuel mixture, had been mentioned. The McLaren involvement with racing at Indianapolis, where the cars run on eye-watering fuel brews, merely added backing to the rumour campaign. The team had received fair warning that their cars would be checked with a fine-tooth comb at Monza, and a fuel check was highly probable in the wake of the press stories. Texaco were naturally aware of this, and became very well aware of it when they encountered entry problems at the Italian frontier. They were held up by patriotic officials for no good reason. The biggest news before Monza was that Niki Lauda had accelerated his recovery and would be leading the Ferrari team at Monza, less than six weeks after a Catholic priest had read the last rites over him in the intensive-care ward. Hunt had talked with Lauda several times on the telephone and was aware that Niki was anxious to be back at the wheel. There were worries over his fitness both mentally and physically. Could he cope with the rigours, the total extension of all his faculties demanded by Formula 1 driving, so soon after his treatment in hospital?

I could understand Niki wanting to get back and race. You have a lot of time to think in hospital, and once he had decided to come back he had to get on with it. He had a terrific amount of motivation too, because he was leading still in the championship and he really wanted to win it. It was a massive stimulus to get back and get stuck in. Here was a challenge and he accepted it.

The stage was set for a tremendous finish to the season with Lauda coming back for Monza. He had missed two races, which meant that he and Hunt had finished exactly the same number of races during the season, and they were within two points of each other.

We were all set for a grandstand finish and then the Italians attacked. We knew that the car would be checked and we knew that fuel would be top of the check list, so we had gone to great pains and precautions in full liaison with Texaco to make absolutely certain that our fuel was legal. When the Italians checked our fuel in the pits on the second day of practice they said it was 101·6 octane. In fact when checked by Texaco in their laboratory it was 101·2 but it didn't matter because you work to units of one octane and we were within the same unit, so that was irrelevant apart from the inefficiency of the checking method. The rule states very simply that you can use the top grade of commercially available fuel in the team's country of origin plus a tolerance of

Heroic return.
Lauda, alone for a
moment, on the
first day of practice
for the Italian Grand
Prix

one octane. Now 101 octane fuel is commercially available in Britain, is registered as such with the FIA and accepted as such by them, which allows us to use 102 octane fuel. In most countries in Europe the top octane is only 100 so that would give a racing allowance for those drivers of 101 octane.

The Italian Automobile Club saw that this ruling could get complicated if they made a fuel check so they had checked with the CSI for a ruling and received a telex in reply from the secretary to the effect that the maximum octane allowed was 101.

This was later to be corrected by a CSI statement, but in the meantime the McLarens were penalized by being put to the back of the grid.

The first two sessions of practice on the Friday had been run in pouring rain and only a few cars went out to try the conditions. Hunt did one lap in the first session and came back with the nose

hanging off his car as a result of spinning off. The Saturday session was fine and it was during this session that the fuel checks were made in the pits. 'I think Ferrari began to believe that if James could beat them, we must be cheating, and they began to try and find excuses', said Teddy Mayer. 'In a way it was beneficial to us because they spent less time on development than perhaps they should have.' Of

The McLaren mechanics pumping a Texaco product at Monza . . .

the other teams, Ferrari's fuel checked out at 98·6 octane, Ligier at 98·6, Lotus at 99·7, Tyrrell at 100·7, McLaren at 101·6, and the Penske team well over at 105·7.

They accepted our notice of appeal against the findings of the fuel check but they still disqualified our practice time from that session – the only one in the dry. They knew there was a chance that we could have the race stripped of its championship status but I'm convinced they thought it would be better to have it dropped than to have me racing from the middle of the pack instead of the back. They knew also that we were unlikely to make so much trouble for them that the race would be dropped from the championship, and they were right.

The McLaren and Penske teams were told that because the fuel check had showed their cars were running on illegal fuel during the Saturday session, times set then would not count for grid positions, but since there was no proof that their fuel had been 'illegal' on the Friday, times set then could be used for the grid; times set in the pouring rain which saw Hunt fifth fastest, Mass seventh and Watson ninth. Set against the dry times on the Saturday, Hunt only just scraped on to the back row of the grid with Mass and Watson as reserves.

One car failed to appear on the morning of the race which let Mass on to the grid, and Guy Edwards withdrew his Penthouse Hesketh which let Watson start on the tail of the grid in his Penske.

While the political drama was being enacted on the Saturday and the Sunday morning in the McLaren and Penske pits, the Ferrari pits were besieged by journalists and photographers determined to capture every word and action of Lauda in his comeback race. The bravery of the man was beyond challenge. The grafted skin around his eyes was angry red, he wore dressings on his head, and his crash helmet had been specially modified to fit. Out of the car he wore a Goodyear cap constantly. It took a special kind of bravery to step back into the public limelight like that; even greater courage to get back into the Ferrari.

For the first time in many many years a French driver in a French car was starting a Grand Prix from pole position – Jacques Laffite in the Ligier-Matra with Jody Scheckter alongside him in the Elf-Tyrrell. On the second row was Carlos Pace in the Martini-Brabham and Patrick Depailler in the other six-wheeler. From the start it was Laffite and Pace in the 12-cylinder cars, but into the first chicane Scheckter was leading. Soon Peterson had joined him and with ten laps gone Peterson's March and the two Elf-Tyrrells were running together in front. Of the 'bad boys' at the back, Mass was in the pits on the second lap with an ignition problem, Hunt was 12th and Watson 14th.

I was last on the first lap after getting stuck in traffic into the bottleneck of the first chicane, but my only chance was to 'charge' and after ten laps I was twelfth, but then I got stuck. It was becoming increasingly difficult to pass people and I was stuck behind Tom Pryce in the Shadow for a bit because he was very quick on the straight, but I eventually got past him and rushed on to catch up to the Belgian Jack Ickx in the Ensign and I had the same trouble with him – only worse. I just couldn't get by. He was too quick for me on the

Following pages:
lonely walk at
Monza

121

straight but he was holding me up through the corners. I was in behind Ickx for a couple of laps and then Pryce caught up again. Going out of the first chicane I missed a gear and Pryce was going to come up alongside me. I could see that, but rather than fight him – we were all in a hurry and wanted to get on with the race – and take the inside line going into the next corner, I took the normal line. But he came hurtling up the inside, outbraking me, racing me into the next corner. That really took me by surprise because if he got past me again all he was going to do was hold both of us up. We would have both gone quicker if he had followed me. I had to fight it out with him then because I'd had a hell of a job passing him already, so I decided to go for it. When we did get to the corner he was inside me, I couldn't get in and I went off the road of my own accord. It was my fault, but at the same time I had to fight. I took the decision when he arrived alongside me to fight him out and it didn't come off. But I still think it was the right decision because had I let go then I would never have finished in the points.

It was a calculated risk. In different circumstances you adjust the size of the calculation. At Monza it was always a risk whether I would finish the race because I had to really try hard. If by half distance you are getting into the points, the first six places, then you adjust yourself and reduce the amount of risk you take because you've got more in the bank to protect.

Hunt had skated off the road into a sand trap, which performed its job of deceleration very effectively and slowed the McLaren so that it just stopped at the first catchfence. Hunt leapt out, checked the car for damage, could find none but was then stopped by marshals from getting back into the cockpit.

They wouldn't let me get back in. They pounced on me. But it wasn't really worth making an issue of it because firstly the car was stuck in the sand and secondly I was now completely out of the race even if I could have re-started. It was then hopeless trying to gain points as far as I was concerned.

On the walk back to the pits, Hunt was hissed and jeered by the crowd, something he had been putting up with all weekend at the track, every time he moved from the shelter of the team's caravan.

The propaganda campaign against me in the Italian Press was really quite incredible, you know. A very heavy deal. Anybody would have thought that it was I who had caused Niki's accident. They really hated me in Italy, to an extent that was quite unbelievable.

Hunt evolved his own way of dealing with the hecklers hanging over the pit fences.

I'd be walking along and they'd all be laughing and hissing but if I swung round suddenly, looked one hard in the eye and said 'boo' at him, he'd immediately smile, go all weak at the knees and thrust out a piece of paper for my autograph . . . pathetic. I was quite pleased to get out of Italy unscathed . . . and I'd managed to avoid getting in a fight with anyone all weekend.

While Hunt was ruminating on his private war with the Italians, Ronnie Peterson was out front in the March winning his third Italian Grand Prix. Regazzoni was second, Laffite third in the Ligier and Lauda fourth, cheered to the echo as he took the flag.

Hunt spoke with admiration of the efforts of his rival.

Niki's race really spoke for itself. To virtually step out of the grave and six weeks later to come fourth in a Grand Prix is a truly amazing achievement, especially as there wasn't much practice time. He just got in the car and had a go. It was bloody good. And he drove a typical Niki race, well-contained within himself and within his new limitation, loosening up for the big battle later. He knew I was out of that race so there was no pressure on him from that point of view. He was just putting a few more points in the bag before he went into battle in earnest. He did a super job . . . a super job.

Peterson had won a fine race in the March and Hunt was moved to say he rated Peterson and Lauda as the best.

They're the two I fear more than anybody, they have abilities that I rate higher than anybody else. They are both absolutely fair. Ronnie is an absolutely straight driver. He doesn't need to do anything silly because he's that good. His physical fitness is perhaps suspect, that's about all. I would think Ronnie's problem is his ability to make the right decisions when he is setting the car up, that sort of thing. You've got to set your car up right to be successful and I don't know whether he can do that as well as some of the others – as well as Niki could or maybe I could. And that would be his potential weakness, far more than any weakness once he's into the race.

When Hunt left Italy he was angry at the way the team had been treated over the fuel check in practice, frustrated because it had pulled the mat from under any chance he might have had to collect points in the race.

We had an appeal in but we all knew that it was a waste of time, and I was frustrated even more when the CSI put out a press release saying that everything was all right and that the McLaren team hadn't been cheating. When people are throwing mud, some sticks. The rules are very complicated and they are difficult to understand. The implication that we had been cheating annoyed me enormously. Not only had we not *been cheating, but running a high octane fuel would not help unless we had increased the compression ratio of the engine to match the increased octane rating. You have to modify your engine accordingly and we certainly hadn't done that – we could have run 150 octane petrol and our engine wouldn't have given an ounce more power. Our fuel was totally legal and we had gone to a lot of trouble before the race to make sure that it was, but to have that understood by the general public was more than one could ask . . . so this mud had been thrown and some of it was inevitably sticking.*

There were three rounds of the championship left and the score was: Lauda 61, Hunt 56. After dinner late that Sunday night Ferrari team manager Daniele Audetto, who confessed his admiration for Hunt, and suggested that the Monza venom had really been intended for McLaren, looked ahead to the last three races of the season. His prognostication was that Hunt would win in the USA, finish second in Canada and third in Japan, which in two cases turned out to be absolutely right. Lauda, he reasoned, would win in Canada, finish second in Japan and fail to score in the USA. In those last three races Regazzoni would finish third, second and first, and that was perhaps the only unrealistic forecast as the team had toasted Clay in the knowledge that he had that day driven his last Grand Prix at Monza in a Ferrari. Audetto's prophesy that Lauda would take the championship by one point from Hunt, 76 to 75, didn't look far from probable, and it took no account of the outcome of Ferrari's protest about the British Grand Prix.

Win Some, Lose Some
Canada

Hunt had flown from Monza to take part in an International Race of Champions contest*, and he went straight on to Toronto for testing and a few days rest rather than flying back to Europe before the Grand Prix at Mosport. His mood was confident, and he thought that there would be a good fight with Lauda until the end of the season – other drivers might have been looking for a cosy points advantage to cruise for the title, but Hunt was looking for a fight.

Niki had a marked advantage at that stage. He was five points up, which was more than enough to be decisive if things were going to be as close as they had been at the start of the season. And I saw no reason why they shouldn't be. Anyway, I was all set to give it a go.

The days between racing are the difficult ones for professional drivers like Hunt, but they tend to enjoy sport and take side benefits from the exercise they get. Hunt sought a squash club in Toronto for a workout on what he knew to be the day of the FIA appeal court hearing on the Ferrari protest over the British Grand Prix. Ferrari alleged that Hunt had not been running at the time the race was stopped after the crash at the first corner, and therefore should not have been allowed to re-start.

I didn't see how they could possibly throw us out because it was an open and shut case as far as the legalities were concerned, but I was a little nervous of the outcome.

When Hunt arrived at the squash club, tight for time and his partner waiting, there was a message to call a Canadian journalist. *The message said would I ring him back about the Paris hearing and to be prepared for bad news. I knew exactly what that meant. News is only good or bad and it was going to be a black or white answer anyway. I didn't call the guy back because I wanted to think about it a bit, so I went to the changing rooms and straight down to the court. I'm pretty tough professionally and it's difficult to move me because I've trained myself to be hard – there's no mileage in letting things upset you. But boy, I couldn't hit that squash ball, I really couldn't concentrate on the game at all. I managed to play . . . I went through the mechanics of playing squash but I've never been on any court or played any game with greater difficulty and less enthusiasm, more mechanically than I did that day. When I came off the court a whole lot of Press people had arrived and they told me the whole thing. It was a very heavy deal.*

Hunt says he never did discover the real reason why he had been thrown out of the British Grand Prix and had his victory taken from

*A short series of races for Grand Prix and US track racing drivers in identical touring cars.

him along with the points in the world championship.

They did put out a garbled message some weeks later but I've never seen it. One of the significant things was that they never said why. *In appeals prior to this they had always stated the findings of the Court and their reasons for finding it, but in this case all they did was issue a result.*

Speculatively there are only two possible reasons. One is that they just plain chose to disbelieve the witnesses, the marshals, the Clerk of the Course and all the people who had been involved in the stopping of the race – the person who put out the directive, when he had put it out, all of which is properly recorded and logged – and the guys out on the track who had given the signals. They could have chosen to disbelieve the witnesses because Ferrari were contending that the race wasn't stopped until after I'd pulled off the track and this just simply wasn't true. They could have disbelieved the RAC witnesses on that or, alternatively, Ferrari were contending if they lost that one, that my intention was to retire. But the rules don't say anything about your intentions. The rule just says that those whose cars are running at the time the race is stopped can re-start and those who aren't, can't. The fact was that my car was running and hadn't retired. I can't see how anyone can talk about a driver's intentions because not even I knew then whether I intended to retire or not and it was totally irrelevant.

This takes me to the thing that really bugs me. If you go back to the Spanish Grand Prix, our car was illegal, inadvertently illegal in a way which did not affect the performance of the car. There was no attempt to cheat or defraud and it was illegal in a similar sort of way to every other Formula 1 car in captivity because the rules are so complicated that no one can build a car legal like that, even the people who try hardest. You can take two attitudes when something is illegal on the car. You can say 'Rules are rules and if you break them, you're out because it's too complicated to decide what's cheating and what isn't!' Or else you can say the rules are far too complicated for that. I mean if an engine is over-size, that's blatant cheating and gaining an advantage and therefore it must be thrown out. But if the one-way valves in the fuel system don't comply, something that is nothing to do with the performance of the car, you get a fine and get told to put it right.

Both attitudes are on the face of it quite defensible, quite reasonable attitudes to take. There's nothing wrong with the first attitude that 'rules is rules'. Let's have it black or white because that's the easiest and simplest way to do it. Good idea. Ferrari, because it suited them, went off on this tangent in a big way, right? But this was a terrible thing for them to do because the Ferrari was illegal during the season.

In Canada it was realized that they had been running their gearbox oil cooler in an illegal position ever since Spain, when the ruling about that came in. Now they weren't trying to cheat or defraud, they had simply not under-stood the rule book properly and put the oil cooler in the wrong place by mistake. This is the problem with the rule book – it's so complicated that things like that are bound to happen on a car. The Ferrari people were hugely embarrassed by this. It wasn't helping their performance any, but you've never seen any-body move anything as fast on a car as they did in Canada when it was pointed out to them! But they had been illegal all year and by their own contention they should have been disqualified for the whole year for that, and that's a pretty stupid contention because we didn't even protest. We wouldn't have dreamed of protesting about them over something like that because it's too silly.

The really important thing about the rules as they stand is this: it is impossible to build a Formula 1 car that will run if you build it exactly to the rules. That's a fact. The safety part of the rulebook dwells, among other things, on the fuel system. The fuel system has various specifications laid down for one-way valves and things in the way you pipe it up. If you build your fuel system to comply exactly to the letter of those rules as the book says, no fuel can get to the engine. That is a fact. It's impossible! Therefore none of the cars in Grand Prix racing has a legal fuel system, but what most of the cars do is to comply with the spirit of the regulations in their one-way valve systems because they've all got them. If you wanted to take every Formula 1 car apart right down to the last nut and bolt and see that it's 100 per cent legal everywhere, you would have to throw every car out. If it moves, you can guarantee that its fuel system isn't legal, and this is where Ferrari are wrong and stupid to take the attitude they did about rules.

The annoying thing to me was that it was all right for Ferrari to be illegal in this way but not all right for anyone else. The main problem was that the rule book always had been open to abuse because of the ineffectiveness of the FIA to deal with the problems and arguments that arose, and to settle them properly and fairly.

It was an exploitation of the rules by Ferrari that hurt everybody. It hurt us, it hurt them and it hurt the sport. It was another nail in the coffin of the FIA as a governing body. It hurt everybody. I can't think of anyone who came out of that episode well. It's an awful pity. I don't want all this hypocrisy and vexation for anybody – even if it's not directed at me – I just don't think it's a good thing. I hope everyone has learnt a lesson and that we can all behave like adults in the future.

Hunt had suffered from the other side of the Atlantic in the furore of the appeal and its result. Looking at the season as a whole, Teddy Mayer thinks the political situation got quite out of hand. 'What happened in Spain was, in my opinion, simply a mistake. A natural one, obviously – or it should be obvious – with no intent to cheat, and the sentence of disqualification was very, very heavy. Too heavy, in our view, and our appeal was upheld. I can understand Ferrari's reaction to that, feeling possibly they should have had the race, but I don't understand the self-righteousness that was then shown by Ferrari in going round and saying that they never broke rules. It's all right to say those things, but to say them and believe them . . . that's something else. We all live in glass houses. No one adheres to the rules absolutely, anymore than anyone adheres to all of the law which is the law of the land absolutely because that's almost impossible. So to display the sort of self-righteousness that Ferrari did seems to me childish.

'The saddest of all was the appeal over the British Grand Prix because James won the race fair and square; there was no question about that, there was no question of his car being illegal. They were trying to use the rules to get out of competing with him and to me that's sad – it really is. OK, the rules are there and you have to adhere to them, but we're also there to entertain the public and we

Among McLaren's rivals in 1976 were the six-wheeled Tyrrells (**top**, Scheckter narrowly leading team mate Depailler) and March (**lower**, Peterson followed by Hunt and Laffite at the Osterreichring) **Following pages:** car preparation in the Marlboro-McLaren team encampment – a scene repeated from paddock to paddock around Europe through the summer

It's a pretty good report in every way. You can't push him into mistakes. He won't take that. He'll do his own thing. He will use the Ferrari power advantage when he needs to. In the Swedish Grand Prix in 1974 he was having a handling problem and I was right up close waiting to get past, but I didn't get through for 40 laps. He didn't hurry around any of the corners because the car was bad but as soon as we got on to the straight he'd put his foot down and go away from me. When I eventually did get past I went away gaining two seconds every lap. That was an extreme example of what Niki does, because he knows. *A lot of other drivers if they had that power advantage and were in Niki's situation, being pressured from behind, they would forget and they'd drive on the limit, in a car not up to being driven on the limit, they'd make a mistake, and just give it away to you. No way will Niki do that because he remembers all the time. So many people forget things, important pieces of information to their own advantage, when they're under pressure. They only think about racing hard, driving fast because it's the only solution and very often it's exactly the wrong solution. Niki would never do that. He's a guy who gets the best out of the situation, he's very tough, he starts well, and finishes consistently. He is totally fair in overtaking. He will always watch for you and if you get alongside he won't barge into you or make contact. He'll make himself as tough as he can to be overtaken in an absolutely fair way, but the moment you're alongside or if you've got the line he won't start doing anything silly which is very important. It means that we always have a clean race together.*

Lauda is 18 months younger than Hunt, but had made his mark faster in Formula 1, by dint of that logical, determined thinking which is one of his strong characteristics. When he decided he was ready for Formula 1 after a conventional apprenticeship in Formula 3 and Formula 2 racing, he arranged sponsorship from an Austrian bank. He had arranged a 'rent-a-drive' when his bankers had second thoughts about their involvement, and backed down. Committed, with a contract to fulfil, Lauda approached another bank with the unlikely proposition that they should put up a sizable sum of money (around £30,000) in return for which he would carry their coat of arms on his car. Banks are not renowned for their sympathetic attitudes towards the dreams of 23-year-old racing drivers, and Austrian banks are more austere than some. Lauda was offered a deal: the money for his life. If Niki would take out a life insurance policy in the sum he required from the bank, with the bank as benefactor, they could do a deal. They did, and Lauda carried the bank's badge all the way to the world championship in 1975. He annexed that championship with five victories.

Clay's alright. He's pretty fierce and you've got to keep clear of him in the opening laps . . . when he is doing his little charge after the start he tends to get a bit erratic, and that's when you're a bit careful. But otherwise he is fine, a good seasoned professional. He can be difficult to get past, but he does know that you are there — you know that if he settles down in a dice he won't do anything silly. There are some drivers who will do silly things in that sort of situation, but Clay's not as bad as people think he is.

should be running our cars in the race, not in some obscure way keeping them out. The sad thing about the Brands Hatch accident was that it was Ferrari's fault – one of their drivers hit the other – and they were trying to take advantage of their own mistakes. To start the new race with a car that was obviously good enough to win, and then have Ferrari say we should never have been in the race at all because of a mistake of theirs, is really bad news. It's cheating the public'.

Up till this point, Hunt and Lauda had been trying to avoid any personal involvement in the political issues. They were the drivers, they were doing their job to the best of their professional abilities, and they were unwilling to transfer team wrangles on to the race track. The issue became personal when the result of the British Grand Prix appeal by Ferrari was announced in their favour and Hunt's victory was thrown out. Lauda was quoted as being delighted at the outcome and when his quotes were relayed to Hunt in Canada, Hunt appeared on British television flaring at Lauda. For the first time, the two men were squaring off at each other rather than leaving the team managers to fight the battles. It was one of those situations when such heated reactions could be expected, almost excused.

A guy brought me round the full wire service report on the appeal that evening and it included a quote from Niki. They had contacted him at home in Austria and asked him what he thought about it. He was quoted as saying that this was a wonderful thing for the sport, the proper thing to do, at last a positive decision had been taken, blah, blah, blah, and generally saying how good it was and how correct the decision was. Which just plain wasn't true and he knew it, right? That made me very cross and I was a bit annoyed with him.

Lauda had also heard quotes from Hunt which angered him, and there was tightrope tension as the teams checked in for the Canadian Grand Prix at the Flying Dutchmen motel near the little country town of Bowmanville, some 45 miles from Toronto.

The drivers were not happy about the state of the Mosport track, a 2½-mile circuit in desolate country ravaged by winter snows every year, which seldom has money spent on maintenance. A deputation from the drivers' safety committee was to meet the organizers, and a wildfire rumour leapt from motel to the organizers, and from motel to motel that Hunt had told Lauda – and these two drivers had most voice on the drivers' safety committee – that he wasn't interested in safety, only in racing. By raceday the rumours had built into a blaze as the reporters did their best to fuel the anger which had flared up between the two drivers for the first time. Hunt says now that purely for reasons of racing tactics he was keen to inflame the situation rather than to cool it down.

I was deliberately trying to make Niki think that I was freaked out, because if he thought I was freaked out by what was happening he would steer clear of me on the track. It was purely a professional piece of gamesmanship, that's all part of the game. If you can 'psych' another driver out and make him frightened of you then he's much easier to pass. I had cultivated the idea with Niki that I was worked up, and without every saying it made him think that

135

*I was going to push him off the track – which was the last thing I'd do . . .
I didn't want to get tangled up with another car because it would probably
send me off the road. But I wanted him to think that way, because after his
accident and everything, if he saw me coming up in his mirrors he'd pull
sharply over and let me through. At least that was my plan.*

On the subject of the safety committee argument, Hunt maintains
he was misquoted. He had told Peter Macintosh, secretary of the
Formula 1 Constructors' Association that he didn't plan on doing
anything further with the safety committee until he had an undertaking that someone was going to sort out the rules and regulations.
*They gave me that undertaking and I'm working with them again. It was
nothing to do with Niki at all. I had decided that I had more than enough on
my plate with the championship and they didn't need me for the last couple of
meetings. It was suggested later that I'd told Niki I didn't care about the
safety in Canada, but I cared very much. What I did say to Niki was that if
the track was in a terrible state – and it was – since he was already going to
sort it all out he didn't need me.*

Hunt had left Monza only five points behind Lauda, but his
paper defeat at Brands Hatch had stretched the gap out to 17 and
severely strained relations between the drivers. *In a way the Canadian
Grand Prix was a race that I least enjoyed and most enjoyed, all at once.*
During practice Hunt had been continually chased by the Press, to
the point where the quietest place he could find was the cockpit of
the McLaren.

By this time I was fired up and wanted to drive, and the only place I could be on my own to get on with the job was in the car. So I enjoyed my driving there more than ever because it was such a super relief. The rest of it I hated.

Practice was fought out between Hunt and Ronnie Peterson in the March, with Hunt taking the pole yet again, this time by four-tenths of a second. Vittorio Brambilla (March) was behind him on the second row, and Patrick Depailler (Elf-Tyrrell) was behind Ronnie. Niki Lauda was sixth fastest on the third row with Mario Andretti.

Hunt had started from the pole yet again, and yet again he was left behind at the start, this time by Peterson. For eight laps he trailed the Swede before moving into the lead. A few laps later Depailler in the six-wheeler nosed through into second place and was fighting close to the McLaren. The little Frenchman who had started the season tangling with Hunt at Long Beach and earning Hunt's extreme displeasure had, in the course of the summer, matured into a driver on the verge of his first Grand Prix win. He was to finish second five times in 1976.

We were always looking good at Mosport, the car ran very well but again suffered from understeer in the race and I had to work hard. Depailler was really giving me a hard time, keeping the pressure on, and if he had got past he was probably capable of running a bit quicker than I was. But he wasn't quite quick enough to attack me. My main worries in Canada were the back markers trailing the field when we came through to lap them, because you only

137

need to do that wrong once and the guy trailing you is through and gone. The back marker moves the wrong way at the wrong moment, you have to brake, and there is a big gap on the other side of the road. So I took great precautions not to let that situation arise. I started playing the back markers against Patrick. I'd cruise, as it were, between groups of back markers because I obviously wasn't going to get away from him, so there was no hurry. Then when we got near the back markers I'd put on a real spurt to get as much air between him and me and to give myself a bit of manoeuvering room. Soon I was timing my arrival with the back markers so that I was ready to pass them at the right part of the circuit. I was giving it real thought and I was managing to get through better than he was, but you need a bit of luck there as well.

The Grand Prix was a cliffhanger, with Depailler as eager to outfox Hunt in the traffic as Hunt was to keep him foxed. A confrontation in the closing laps – in a situation like this the real and final pressure always comes in the closing ten laps – was averted when Depailler began to drop back inexplicably. He crossed the line some six seconds adrift, braked to a sudden halt after taking the flag, staggered out of the car and collapsed against the rear wheel almost overcome by petrol fumes. A special petrol-filled safety diaphragm was built into the fuel system behind the cockpit so that the fuel pressure gauge on the instrument panel did not have to be fed by a petrol line. These fuel lines in the cockpit had ruptured or punctured in the past and caused serious problems for the driver. In this instance Depailler's safety system had malfunctioned, a freak occurrence that probably cost him the race. He said afterwards he had been driving like a drunk, taking each corner as it came, not sure exactly where he was on the track. He felt as though he had drunk a bottle of whisky, and the padded lining of his helmet was saturated with petrol.

Niki Lauda had been running fifth for much of the race behind Hunt, Depailler, Andretti and Scheckter, but before the end he had dropped to eighth place with a problem in the rear suspension of the Ferrari. It was his second race since his accident in Germany and he was still working his way back to form.

Hunt may have been consciously playing the publicized rift between himself and Lauda to advantage but there comes a point in any psychological confrontation such as this when it is difficult to isolate the truth from the tactics. The two drivers realised it would be better if they discussed their differences before the thing got completely out of hand, and after the race at Mosport they spent some time together. Lauda insisted that he had never said the things he'd been quoted as saying after the announcement from Paris that Hunt had lost the British Grand Prix. And Hunt was able to deny quotes that Lauda had heard attributed to him. So the hatchet was buried. The two men knew where they stood again, and the points situation had swung in favour of Lauda again. While in winning Hunt had only made up for the nine which the FIA had taken away, Lauda had gained three because of his promotion to winner of the British Grand Prix.

Watkins Glen
the Longest Odds

Before the Canadian Grand Prix my chances of winning the championship must have been 20 to 1 against. I was 17 points behind Lauda, which meant that I had to take 18 points from the final three Grand Prix without Niki scoring. Even if he hadn't been turning up at the races he was still clear favourite to take the title because 18 points is more than most drivers score in a season, let alone in three races. If I had had one retirement, it meant I had to win the other two races to win the championship by one point – even if Niki hadn't bothered to come . . .

It was really too much to do, so by Watkins Glen I wasn't too bothered about the championship, but I hadn't given it up completely because while there's life there's hope. I could only knuckle under and go after each race as it came and try to win it. If I couldn't win I had to finish as high as I could.

Watkins Glen is a sleepy little tourist town on the Seneca Lakes in upstate New York, a morning's drive from the Canadian border. The teams stay either in the Glen Motor Inn or the Seneca Lodge. The drivers tend towards the Motor Inn and the mechanics stay where the evening action is, at the Lodge. The Franzese family has run the Motor Inn for as long as there has been racing on the Glen track, and the drivers and journalists are regarded almost as extensions of a large family. It is one of the few times during the season when most of the Grand Prix grid sits down to breakfast in the same dining room. If there is a problem it is quickly felt around the room because there are no secrets at the Glen. When the competition to sign drivers was particularly tense at the end of one season, the journalists would sit up in the dining room looking out from the picture windows over the lake and the motel buildings below, logging the movements of drivers between the rooms of the different team managers.

The Glen circuit is laid out on higher ground beyond the town, some ten minutes' drive from the motels or a ten-dollar flip in a helicopter on race morning. Usually the 3·3-mile circuit has held the key to the world championship, as its final round, but in 1976 the finale was to be in Japan, at the foot of Mount Fuji.

Hunt was on pole position again, fastest in practice for the eighth time, pace-maker at over half the tracks, and beside him was Jody Scheckter in the Elf-Tyrrell six-wheeler. In Sweden the six-wheelers had finished first and second, and they had been contesting the lead at Monza and Mosport. At Watkins Glen Scheckter was to be Hunt's main opponent in one of his final drives for the Tyrrell team before leaving to lead a new team for Austrian-born Canadian, Walter Wolf.

By the end of the season the six-wheelers seemed to be getting better; they were starting to get the best out of the new design. One of our major problems with Formula 1 cars these days is understeer with full tanks, and this understeer is a killer for speed. It just slows you, and I think the Tyrrells with their six-wheel configuration may have suffered less than we did in this. It certainly looked like that in Canada, where Depailler didn't have a front-end grip problem and just about everybody else did.

But there's nothing special about the six-wheelers. They seem to go very well but they don't go super well, and as yet they've done nothing that you can't do with a four-wheeled car. As far as I can see they can't really do any better because their performance is governed by the size of the rear tyres, and unless they can get more grip at the back they can't use the potential extra grip at the front. The original idea wasn't that anyway, it was to improve it aerodynamically, to get the front wheels down out of the airstream by replacing the normal-sized front wheels with four little ones, and that doesn't really seem to have worked. It hasn't been super quick on the straights this year, so I can't really see the point. When the car has reached the end of its development life they have either got to take the theory substantially further or go back to having a car with four wheels. I don't see that there's a future for them or anyone else building a six-wheeler to the configuration they've got at the moment.

Hunt had been on pole position eight times but the only start he had won was from the re-start in Germany when he was alone on the front row of the grid. Watkins Glen was no exception. *I actually made quite a good start, but Jody made a super one.* Scheckter stormed off into the lead and it was to be past half distance before Hunt could reel him in.

It was an interesting situation for me and it taught me something about my driving. Normally you get in the car and set off in practice, and by race time you know the car and the track so well that when the race starts and you're through the first lap, you switch on to 'auto-pilot' and you put your concentra-

Jody Scheckter
holding a narrow
lead over Hunt in
the US Grand Prix
at Watkins Glen

*tion on to the race, the more total and general picture, because your driving –
the physical act of getting the car around the track quickly – is automatic.*

*After about ten laps at Watkins Glen I realized I was driving like an old
grandmother. Jody was about three seconds up on me and I was holding the
gap, so there was no problem about that, no danger that he would disappear
into the distance, but I wasn't closing on him either, and I ought to have been.
Niki was seven seconds behind me in third place and was holding that gap,
so it could have gone either way – he might have gained or lost – and I couldn't
afford to take the risk that he was going to get quicker. It took me another
few laps to realize what was happening with my driving and then to get it
together. The car was oversteering which made it quick but difficult to drive,
but I was driving like an old woman because I wasn't concentrating on the
physical act of driving.*

*I was making mistakes around the track and I had to spend five laps learning
it all over again, concentrating purely on the driving and nothing else. Eventually after 20 laps I was driving OK again. But it took me 20 laps to get
driving decently and it was a big lesson to me. I came out of it unscathed because nobody overtook me and my race position didn't suffer, and as Jody was
going as quick as I wanted to go at that stage anyway, I wasn't being held up.*

*I was most unhappy with myself because I really drove rather badly, but 18
months earlier I would have set off like that, driven the whole race like that
and never realized that I was driving badly. . . . The important thing to me
is that I was able to pinpoint the fact that I was driving badly and do something about it. This is important in all walks of life, to be able to catch yourself when you're doing something badly and to make sure you improve.*

*So I got myself together. We had lost Niki, and by a third of the distance
there were just two of us. I was going well now but I couldn't get close to Jody
for the same reason Patrick couldn't get close to me in Canada. By half
distance it was obvious that I could go quicker than Jody but I couldn't get
close enough to have a stab at him.*

The only place at the Glen where you could get set up to pass was to get right behind someone going through the chicane before the straight and then pass them on the straight. My car was quick because it was 'oversteery' but it was doing it too much, and it was really 'evil' on two corners. The problem was they were the two most important corners – the corner on to the pit straight and the corner off it. Because I was so slow through those two corners I had always fallen too far behind Jody to pass him by the time we arrived at the chicane. I would be right with him round the back of the track, round through the woods, but then I'd lose all the distance I'd gained when we got to those two corners.

Eventually he got held up going into the chicane by a backmarker and I found myself just the right distance behind, so that I could get a run through without lifting, and I blew past him on the straight. I was gone then. I knew I had to make up a time cushion of some seconds lead in case the same thing happened to me with a slower car. And that's exactly what happened!

Hunt was leading on the 40th lap by a bare two seconds, not enough to be called commanding but enough for each driver to know the score: Hunt would win unless something untoward occurred. As he headed into the chicane the dark blue Williams car in front of him slowed dramatically. It was the Australian driver Warwick Brown in his first Grand Prix, soldiering slowly on, having lost third and fifth gears and his rear brakes. The slow car threw Hunt off his stride.

This guy virtually came to a stop right in the middle of the chicane. It was too slow for third gear and my car was going chug-chug-chug, slowing down as I came out of the chicane, so I started fumbling around trying to get into first. In that sort of situation there is always a danger that you will snatch at gears, so I snatched and missed.

By now Jody was on my heels and he blasted past me on the straight. I really thought I'd blown it then, because I'd needed the help of back markers to get past him the first time and you don't get help like that twice in a race. If I was going to get past Jody again, I was going to have to muscle my way through, but I was doubtful about that because it meant getting tangled up in the turbulence of his rear wing.

As Hunt had discovered very early in his career, rear wing efficiency is vital to counter the lift of the car and to balance it. The wing needs a clear airstream to operate at its maximum efficiency, but the wing creates a turbulence behind it that plays havoc with the nose wings of the following car. These short, broad trim tabs either side of the nose also operate in clear air, but in turbulence they are robbed of their efficiency. Thus a following car instantly develops unpredictable handling characteristics that make driving a nightmare.

I knew that if I could just get past Jody I would be away for a win. The adrenalin was pumping, and it was the old calculated risk being run up the pole again. I had to get close and just drive on the ragged edge until I could get a passing opportunity. Finally I was close enough at the chicane to suck out of his slipstream on the straight, and then I was alongside him and away. I was through then and I made sure I didn't get tangled up with back markers again . . .

The friendship between Hunt and Scheckter is unusual in such a fiercely competitive sport. Hunt tends to have a small circle of close friends, enjoying the company of those he knew before he started racing more than that of the men he races with and against. Jody Scheckter is his closest friend among the drivers. It was Hunt who coined the nickname 'Fletcher' for Scheckter from the gull of the same name in the book 'Jonathan Livingstone Seagull', who was initially over-anxious about flying and kept crashing.

I suppose I got to know Jody very well when he was living in Spain. In fact it was only just before he left to live in Monte Carlo that I started to get to know him properly, and it was a source of sadness to me that he left when he did. Jody is quite a defensive sort of person and it was probably professional rivalry that inhibited the forming of our friendship. We're now very good friends but we missed the opportunity, it formed too slowly. If we had been as good friends then as we are now, I think he would have stayed in Spain. But he didn't know many people down here. He wasn't having much fun, so he left.

I like Jody because he has an exceptional intelligence and wit. He's very funny. But it takes him a long time to get it out because he's not an educated guy. Because of his intelligence he was aware that he lacked education. He felt he was at a disadvantage, and therefore he was very defensive, but he's got over that now. He's got his confidence. I like people with good minds, I find it stimulating, and Jody has an exceptionally sharp brain.

Because of his friendship, Hunt was concerned not to appear to be offering undue criticism:

I'm worried about Jody's driving because although he is capable of being as good as anybody, he hasn't consistently produced this year, which is either because he couldn't set the car up properly or because Ken [Tyrrell] wouldn't let him. I think he was being inhibited because Ken wanted to do what Patrick [Depailler] said all the time and it wasn't necessarily what Jody wanted. So he couldn't give of his best consistently and therefore his performances were disappointing, really, in that he'd go well sometimes and other times he wouldn't go well at all. You can't be sure whether it was him or the team, of course, but it was happening anyway.

He obviously has the ability and the talent, but with the Wolf deal I wondered if he had gone for the money instead of the best drive. Mind you, I don't know whether there were obvious championship-winning drives available to him. I'm not decrying the Wolf team, because it may be very good – it certainly has the people and the finance, but I did wonder at the time if he had chosen the right team, because a new team has got to be a risk – cohesion is everything when you're going for the championship, and this cannot be guaranteed when starting from scratch.

To the surprise of virtually everybody in racing, Scheckter won the first Grand Prix of 1977 in a Wolf – the new team turned out to be very competitive in the first races of its first season.

Hunt did not tangle with any more back markers through those closing laps – indeed, in a clear run to the flag he set a new lap record for the circuit, while Scheckter drifted back to finish eight seconds behind. Lauda fought increasing understeer in his Ferrari to fend off last-minute attacks on his third place by Jochen Mass. He picked up four valuable points; there was one round left, and the score was Lauda 68, Hunt 65.

Against All Odds
Japan

The rain was drifting in again. Not heavy but persistent. Out on the track you could see men with brooms trying to clear the worst of the puddles. From time to time fog (actually low cloud) moving in around the foot of Mount Fuji, rolled in and hid the sweepers from view. Watching the dismal scene from the first floor of the control tower the Grand Prix drivers, team managers and the organizers of the Japanese Grand Prix worried back and forth about starting the final and most important race of the season. The irony that the race which held the key to the efforts of drivers in 15 previous races should be confined to a characterless circuit devoid of challenge, was lost on the men who would soon be racing on it. The rain overnight and during the morning had added the element of danger from blinding spray and from the chilling loss of grip when tyres ski on pools of water at 180 mph.

Aside from the arguments that had broken out here and there as race time had come and gone, Niki Lauda and James Hunt, prince and pretender, debated their position. Both men were winners, Grand Prix fighters who knew what it took and what it meant to win, but they were both prepared to concede the fight in Japan to the weather. Perhaps they could come back and race the next day . . . or the next weekend. As the champion, Lauda had his responsibilities to the sport, but he was a different Niki Lauda from the man who had won as he pleased in 1975. It was only two months since his faithful Ferrari had turned into an inferno at the Nürburgring, and Lauda owed his life to the courage of his fellow drivers who dragged him from the wreckage of his car. There were those who said some of Lauda's iron nerve had eroded, that he now knew, and knew better than anyone else, what it could take to kill you on a race track. Lauda the automaton, the mechanical man who bolted himself into his Ferrari and went out to win, now had a soul. Victory wasn't his most consuming goal anymore. Life was. James Hunt looked at life another way. He enjoyed his. The races were an activity he had done every second weekend during the summer. Between times, life was for living. Of these two men at the top of their profession with personalities poles apart, one by the end of the afternoon would be world champion. But now they discussed quietly and privately whether they should race. Hunt told Lauda that he personally felt they should wait and race another day, but that if the race was started, if the cars were ordered to the grid, he would race. He wouldn't race hard, he wouldn't dispute the issue with the handful of hard drivers who were all for racing anyway, but he would set his own pace. Lauda was now in a corner, literally with his back to the wall, while out on the terraces the Japanese fans huddled under umbrellas wondering what all the delay was about.

For some drivers there was no soul searching; if they searched any souls the souls belonged to the drivers who were reluctant to race. The March drivers were anxious to get at it – Ronnie Peterson, Vittorio Brambilla and Hans Stuck. Drivers who lived and raced on the razor edge. Tom Pryce, the talented Welshman hovering on the verge of his first win, wanted to race. 'We're paid all this money and we're supposed to be the best drivers in the world. We should be able to handle a few puddles.' Alan Jones agreed. His father had won the Australian Grand Prix and the New Zealand Grand Prix in the early 1950s, and the handsome young Australian was preserving family tradition. He put his vote in to race the factory Surtees car, come what may.

The race stewards took the decision away from the drivers. The race was delayed but it would start. Relieved of decisions and responsibilities, perhaps fearful of what the race in the rain would hold in store for them, the drivers filed down out of the tower and hurried to their pits. The curtain was about to go up on the final act of a play that had started ten months earlier in Brazil and followed a completely improbable script around the world to end with a showdown in Japan. If James Hunt was to win the Japanese Grand Prix he would win the world championship. Other permutations could also give him the title, but there were also short-odds permutations that meant Lauda could keep his crown.

Tension bordered on the impossible as cars were fired up in the pit lane, an alley of blasting power, mechanics with ear protectors, drivers dragging flame resistant balaclava hoods over their heads, then forcing down the all-enveloping crash helmets. Even on the grid the start was delayed again, but now it was down to minutes and not hours. Team managers looked up at the lowering skies threatening early darkness that could curtail the race and decide the championship. There were worries in the pits that the wet race would trigger accidents and worse as the drivers released their pent-up tensions along with all that horsepower on the puddle track. But others reasoned that wet races were statistically safer, that if there were accidents they happened at lower speeds.

Suddenly, almost before the pits were aware of it, the race was on. Immediate leader was the red McLaren driven by Hunt, spearing into the murk, winning the gamble for the front and piling on a lead as the cars behind ploughed into a curtain of spray. Already the championship looked settled. There was Hunt impossibly far in front, but where was Lauda who had qualified third in practice? He was drifting back through the pack, blind in the spray, being passed on all sides as back markers forced their way through. It was sad to see, sadder still when Lauda dropped off the chart altogether after two laps and stopped at his pit. For the first time in his Grand Prix career he had given up. He had been unable to see, but his sight problem was aggravated by a legacy of his Nürburgring burns. He

You've got to admire him right from the start for the very fact that he's in Formula 1, because he had a perfectly good living in the States, he had been very successful and had everything going for him. He wanted the new challenge of Formula 1, and it must be rather like going back to school. There is less money in it, too, but it was what he wanted to do and I admire him enormously for it.

Despite his years, I think he improved in 1976. He's got a fantastic amount of experience, he's a racer of the old type who like to get out and race, he's a competitor – he like's to compete and win.

Mario is a real charger. He can be quite rough in the early laps, and I got the impression up to the middle of 1976 that every time there was an incident – like a couple of cars tangling in a Grand Prix – you would always find Mario at the bottom of the pile. It was never his fault – he never seemed to cause incidents, but he always seemed to be involved in them – perhaps because he was driving too near the limit and hadn't left himself that little bit in reserve to get round trouble other people had started.

He has really settled intb Formula 1, now that he has got the experience of Grand Prix racing. He always could drive as fast as anybody, but driving fast is one thing and consistently winning or getting the results is another thing in every formula. I know that I could not expect to go back into Formula 3 and consistently win races; I would have to get the feel of it again, and learn the specialist business. Mario has done his Grand Prix schooling now, and I reckon he is very good.

Forgotten winner. In the excitement of Hunt's third place, the fact that Mario Andretti won the Japanese Grand Prix was almost overlooked.
In the spring of 1977 he was overjoyed to become the first American driver to win an American Grand Prix when he gained a seven-tenths of a second victory over Niki Lauda at Long Beach

couldn't blink his eyes and this was upsetting his focusing. But above all that, Niki Lauda knew that his life meant more than a second season with the world title, and he didn't mind if the world knew it. He sat on the pit counter, his decision made and dramatically announced.

On the track, conditions were improving with every lap. A breeze had sprung up to clear clouds and rain. It was also drying the track. Having set up a buffer lead of several seconds, Hunt shrugged off challenges from Brambilla's March, and then settled out ahead of his team mate, Jochen Mass. For the McLaren men it was a repeat of the German GP when they had dominated the mountain track in the rain. On the pit counter Niki Lauda was thinking the same thing – it was the race that had nearly killed him.

So the championship was all over bar the shouting. Or was it? Now the drama was shifting to a different area. If it had centered on the rain and spray before, it was now bearing on the fact that the track was drying and drying fast. The field had started on grooved wet-weather tyres, Goodyears with treads as opposed to slicks. The drying track meant accelerated wear on the wet-weather tyres as the heat built up. Drivers who knew were deliberately seeking the still-wet areas of the track to keep down the temperatures; drivers who didn't were being signalled so to do by their pits. Hunt had been conscious of the tyre problem and said he had eased the pace after 15 laps to conserve his rubber. Andretti had wondered why Hunt seemed to stay in the dry areas.

With the race two-thirds run and Hunt a confident leader, the championship seemed settled. But now the pit wall watches were showing a change in the pattern. Hunt was slowing and Patrick Depailler was hauling him in dramatically. As the McLaren went past on the broad straight you could now see the car down on one side, as it breasted a bump each lap there were sheets of sparks from the underside. Hunt's left rear tyre was deflating. Now it was a gamble. Would he stop and change the tyre? Would his pit signal him in to change? Could they afford the 20-odd seconds the change would take? Even though Lauda had opted out of the race, he still stood to keep his title if Hunt finished lower than fourth. A pit stop to change the sagging tyre could so easily pitch him out of the points, altogether.

It was an untenable situation for team manager Teddy Mayer. Whatever he did could be the wrong decision. It seemed wiser not to make one. Depailler moved into the lead and pulled away for two laps and then fell off his commanding pace as he weaved past the pits, ten laps left, with a punctured rear tyre. Now Andretti had inherited the lead in the Lotus and Hunt was second. Fate was kinder to Hunt. As he came off the last corner his left front tyre let go, the wet-weather cover simply worn out at the pace required to lead on a dry track. He swung for the pit lane, the McLaren team mechanics who had been anxiously waiting for lap after lap fell on the car, threw on a new set of 'wet' tyres in less than half a minute, and Hunt was wheel-spinning back into the race.

Now Hunt was a different man. The calculating tactician had been replaced by a racer with a red mist of anger descending. How could he have blown the title like that? He cursed the tyres and cursed his luck. Cursed also the pit signal that told him he was sixth because it wasn't only sixth, it was 'goodbye world championship'. In a mounting fury, Hunt slammed round those closing laps, caution cast to the winds, and it was this infuriated charge, this lunge at the whole desperate season, that carried Hunt back into the world championship. Almost without realizing it he passed Clay Regazzoni's Ferrari and Alan Jones' Surtees, the pair battling for

Pit stop of the year. The McLaren mechanics changed all four wheels on Hunt's M23 in 27 seconds when the race at the Fuji International Speedway had five laps to run. Hunt rejoined in fifth place

third place on now-bald tyres. Hunt swept down the short hill at the back of the pits and simply drove round the outside of them on the tight left-hander, the only slow corner on the track.

The tension in the pits defied description. Team managers, and lap charters renowned for their cool heads under fire, had their race strategy fall apart. It was impossible that Hunt could have rejoined the race 'without a prayer to save him' and suddenly be in there racing for the lead again. Signals flashed over the pit wall without anyone being exactly sure what they meant. And now the chequered flag was out and three cars were coming up from that last turn as a single blur. Surely the lead wasn't to change on the line! Andretti in the black Lotus, Depailler in the blue six-wheeler and Hunt in the Marlboro-McLaren. Blat-blat-blat, as fast as that they crossed the line in first, second and third places; and only afterwards when the excitement had evaporated did people realize that Depailler

Right: Hunt on his way to a crucial maximum points score in Canada . . . and (**following pages**) splashing his way to a nail-biting – and even more crucial – third place in the Japanese Grand Prix

Sweetest moment.
Hunt climbs out of
his cockpit after the
last race of 1976,
finally convinced by
Mayer and a forest
of three-finger
gestures that he had
finished third in the
Japanese Grand
Prix and gained the
World Champion-
ship of Drivers by a
single point

and Hunt were a lap down on Andretti after their pit stops. It didn't seem to matter. But it mattered a lot to James Hunt. He was the only man at the track who didn't know he was world champion. He came down the pit lane blipping the throttle, furious and ready to vent that fury . . . His burning wish was to blast team manager Teddy Mayer for the lack of decision on the tyre signals. Why hadn't they told him to come in when they knew his tyre was going down? Why did they tell him he was sixth one lap and third the next?

He braked to a stop at the pit, not caring, perhaps unaware of the crowd that surged around as he wrestled out of the safety harness and dragged himself from the cockpit, shouting so that Mayer could

hear him through the bar of his Bell Star helmet. By this time Mayer, who had moved in to congratulate his new world champion, was switching delight to concern under the verbal barrage, a sudden victim of the 'short fuse'. As Hunt pulled his helmet off and paused for breath, Mayer quietly told him that he had finished third and was world champion. Hunt believed him and didn't believe him. He wanted to hear that he was champion but didn't want to believe it in case that sweet smell of success was dragged from him, as had happened so often during the year. The surge of mechanics, journa-lists and hangers-on were shouting their congratulations at the new champion but he was reluctant to hear them. *I wanted proof*, he said later and it wasn't until he had checked other lap charts and had it officially confirmed by the race organizers without protests from other teams, that James Simon Wallis Hunt believed himself to be the 1976 World Champion racing driver.

The World's Most Famous Hangover

When the chequered flag fell in the rapidly gathering dusk to mark the end of the Japanese Grand Prix at the Mount Fuji circuit on October 24 1976, there were separate pockets of celebration in the pits. The John Player Lotus team were spilling over the pit wall into the track to cheer their number one driver, Mario Andretti, who had snatched the lead ten laps from the end to win the race he had started from pole position. Theirs was a celebration born almost of relief at having grabbed a win before the end of the season, for there is a chill feeling of inadequacy about a team – a top team – that runs a full season without a win.

In the Marlboro-McLaren pit you couldn't see James Hunt and his car for people. Hunt had scrambled in third, but he had clinched the world championship, and everyone pressed congratulations on him when all he wanted was confirmation. *Two laps from the end of the last race . . . it must have been the latest the World Championship has ever been decided,* said Hunt at his home in Spain a couple of weeks later. In fact there had been a precedent in 1964 when, on the very last lap of the last race in the series, Italian Ferrari driver Lorenzo Bandini was signalled to slow and hand over his second place to British team-mate John Surtees, who gained enough points by the manoeuvre to clinch the championship. Hunt was sick with worry after all the disappointments, protests, changes and disqualifications during the season.

I was absolutely determined not to think that I was world champion and then get disappointed, because there were 300 good reasons why something should have gone wrong. It was only really when I checked the laps and when the organizers said I was third – and there were no protests in the wind – that I allowed myself to start believing it. I mean I still didn't feel that good when they put me up on third place on the rostrum because I wasn't sure I wasn't going to be dragged off there at the last minute. . . So the championship win came to me slowly.

He was soon deep in interviews – *the usual interviews only longer now, and more of them* – and it struck Hunt that he was glad he had taken the title in Japan and not in Europe, where the crowds of journalists, radio and television commentators would have turned the press conference into a battlefield.

It would have been completely impossible for me in Europe, but in Japan and so far from home I knew most of the people I had to deal with after the race, the Press regulars who travel the circuits with us, so that made it easier. The Japanese really had no idea what was going on. They were running a motor race and enjoying the fact. They were amused that so many of these funny westerners seemed to be getting so excited about it, but beyond that I don't think they had a clue. Obviously a small contingent of Japanese racing enthusiasts knew exactly what was going on, what was at stake, and they certainly weren't creating a hassle.

The narrow roads around the foot of Mount Fuji, some 60 miles from Tokyo, meant that the traffic was jammed solid after the race, and the Grand Prix 'circus' – the nomadic group of perhaps 300 who attend every race around the world, and include drivers, managers, mechanics, journalists and sponsors – stayed on in the darkness as the mechanics packed cars and spares for the long haul back to Europe in the belly of an aircraft, the Press hammered out the news of the championship and the race in their operations centre, and James Hunt began to celebrate, slowly at first. A beer with his mechanics, congratulations all round after a hard season, and then relaxation in the Champion spark plug hospitality pit, a haven of congeniality far from the luxury of the motorhomes which most teams use as their track headquarters during European race week-ends. The 1976 World 500cc Motorcycle Champion Barry Sheene and Hunt talked together in the pit. Hunt was resting, relaxing, unable to leave the track because of the traffic, wanting to stay anyway.

It's a matter of principle with me now, staying at the track after the race. It was a Hesketh Racing rule – 'Bubbles' Horsley always had a lot of rules and ideas on how things should be about team and team spirit – for me not to leave after a race, but to stay and leave on the Monday morning. I would always stay and have a drink with the lads, and I think it's a jolly good rule because I enjoy it.

A flaw in Hunt's image as the ideal racing champion is that he doesn't like champagne: *I don't really like champagne, and especially not right after a race. I prefer a beer to quench my thirst and I'll take wine with a meal from time to time.*

The dining room at the Mount Fuji circuit closed religiously at nine o'clock every night. At 8.45 on the night after the Grand Prix it was empty. At nine on the stroke, as if by magic, it was full. The Marlboro-McLaren table was in high spirits and champagne coolers kept arriving.

The Marlboro party had been adroitly pre-planned as a celebration whichever driver won, since Hunt was Marlboro-sponsored and Lauda had a personal sponsorship deal with Marlboro as one of their World Championship team of international sportsmen. The tobacco company was a generous host and turned a blind eye as the mechanics souvenired bottles of gin, spiriting them out of the Hilton under their coats. If it had been a merciful release from a long hard season for their drivers, the mechanics were no less jubilant, and relieved. The drivers inevitably enjoy the limelight while the mechanics work as the underside of the iceberg. Now, with the season over and the championship won, they were coming up for air, and were to provide much of the light-hearted relief on the long and gruelling trip over the North Pole back to England aboard the Japan Air Lines Boeing 747.

The new champion
mobbed by
autograph-seekers
at the London
Motor Show the
day after his return
from Japan

When the 747 nosed into the terminal at London Airport it was the season's end for most people, but for Hunt it meant a startling change of pace. Ranks of photographers greeted him at the ramp, and his family and friends were waiting to meet him beyond Customs.

When we got to London I wasn't feeling too bad – a bit shattered, but my mind was still working. I wasn't feeling ill, just exhausted. My family was there as well as the Press, and that threw me completely. I hadn't expected my family to be at the airport and that was the most unnerving thing, having to say hello to them in front of 2000 people. It was a bit of a heavy deal, with mother freaking out and everything; that's what really threw me. The Press conference was a brief ordeal, but it was an ordeal. It was overwhelming. In most situations I feel in control but when I get out of control I'm not sure whether I'm doing or saying the right thing. Not because of what people want to hear, so much as the difficulty of what I want to say to them. That sort of thing makes me feel uncomfortable.

With the Press conference behind him he was whisked off with his friends to a champagne breakfast in the flat where his friend and companion of the moment, secretary Jane Birbeck, was staying with her sister and brother-in-law.

Finally it all packed up about lunchtime and I crashed asleep, right there. I slept for a bit in the afternoon and then for a few hours in the evening before going out to dinner. That was Tuesday. On Wednesday morning I went in to the office with Peter and in the afternoon I had another session of television and newspaper interviews. I was booked on the 9 o'clock flight to Malaga that night and I nearly missed it. Iberia, the Spanish airline, are very good to me in London and they held the flight a few minutes. I know they can't do that officially, but if they hadn't held the plane they would have been 50 per cent short on payload since two newspaper reporters were travelling with me and there were only six passengers in total on the DC9 that night.

On summer schedules the late flight to Malaga gets in at one o'clock in the morning, a dead hour in the damp warmth of the Spanish riviera. But the airport was alive with friends who had set up yet another champagne party at the Customs exit. It was an hour back to his house and nudging dawn when he arrived to more partying, more congratulations from neighbours and friends. For two days he rested and on the late night plane on Friday his friends from home arrived for the weekend. After seven days of celebrations, the mere driving of the Grand Prix must have seemed the easiest part of winning the World Championship.

In the hectic weeks before Christmas there were only a few days at home in Marbella for Hunt, and a few days testing the M26 at the Paul Ricard circuit. The rest of his time belonged to his sponsors, and to the off-season round of racing presentations and shows, commuting around Europe. He returned to Italy for the first time since the Grand Prix for the annual *Autosprint* presentations and a totally different welcome:

I was the villain at Monza, but when I went back after I had won the championship you would have thought I was the biggest hero ever to come into Italy. After the presentation at Bologna, I went next door to Agostini's show, and the 20 police we had couldn't control the crowd, who were breaking the place down trying to get at me – for friendship. We had only been in there two minutes when the police said 'you've appeared, you had better go now'. I sympathize with the Italian crowds – they treat racing like a religion, get very passionate, and are fed a complete load of rubbish by their Press.

A less happy Italian episode came in Milan the following day. While Hogan and Hunt were attending an official Philip Morris lunch, their car was emptied of their belongings, Hunt losing some of his awards, his passport, cheque books, credit cards, travellers cheques, diary and address books, while both lost the Polish visas which they were scheduled to use the following day.

The Italian police did not seem interested, and the British consul was not able to help much, so we left Italy 'illegally' the following morning, and luckily were able to get new passports and visas in Geneva. The most annoying loss turned out to be the diary, which contained the exact dates and times of my visits to the UK, which meant that I had to sit down and try to reconstruct the last year for the tax man.

The pressures began to ease towards the end of December. Hunt makes no bones about the fact that he is not keen on making speeches and obviously prefers to be his own man – at times, the short fuse had appeared to be smouldering.

I had guessed that I would be busy, but I never really thought it would be possible to squeeze so much into such a short time – those two months were the most hectic of my life. I have never been so relieved to get to my home and my dog, and I had a very quiet Christmas as I started working up towards Argentina and Brazil.

I am still very new to this. Everybody is gunning for you if you are on top, and the massive invasion of privacy is worse than being at school. My personal freedom is something I had worked for so long, and it seemed that just as I was getting it, it was sort of removed . . .

Number One
Into a New Season

A year earlier, James Hunt had flown to South America as a new boy in the McLaren team. For the 1977 season opener in Argentina he was returning as world champion.

The Argentine Grand Prix was cancelled in 1976 because of political problems within the country. The race came close to cancellation in 1977 because of political problems outside Argentina, problems that involved the governing body of the sport, and a company that had been formed to negotiate on behalf of race organizers with the various teams. A few days before Christmas it was finally agreed that the race would be held as scheduled on January 9.

Temperatures hovered around 100 degrees in the pit lane, in open parkland on the outskirts of Buenos Aires, with the mercury climbing over 120 degrees above the track surface. Armed troops and special police were everywhere. These were not examples of the normal Latin cop, with a pistol on his hip that would probably blow his hand off if he ever dared to pull the trigger – in Argentina the soldiers were carrying automatic rifles, submachine guns, riot shotguns, tear gas, and assorted light artillery on troop and weapon carriers. All cars entering the circuit were stopped each day and searched at gunpoint. The fear was that extremist groups in Argentina might use the Grand Prix as an international platform for disruption, and with the new government less than a year old and a cost of living figure that had just climbed by over 300 per cent in that period, there were no allowances made for professional troublemakers.

Another major cause for concern was the World Cup football series due to be played in Argentina in 1978. If the Grand Prix was disrupted by violent demonstrations, the chances of the World Cup being staged would be slim.

The McLaren M23 was being brought out again for its fifth season of Grand Prix racing while the new M26 model stayed at the Colnbrook factory in Britain. The new car was still being developed, and a decision was made to take a pair of M23s for Hunt and Jochen Mass rather than endure the complicated logistics of fielding two totally different cars.

We ran into a special kind of problem with getting the M26 off the ground. Most teams introduce a new car because they bloody well need it and therefore are prepared to speculate, to chuck the old car away and get on with the new car on the theory that the old car wasn't good enough and even if it means struggling with the new car for a couple of races, it's a good investment. We

Number One. Hunt
in his faithful
McLaren M23/8
in the 1977
Argentine Grand
Prix . . .

were faced with the problem of trying to run two completely different cars – the M23 and the M26 – with a team that's big enough to run only one type at a time. We have only been able to snatch the odd day of testing with the M26 when we can afford 'days off' from the racing programme with the M23, and this makes the development programme slower than perhaps it should be. So in South America we were committed one hundred per cent to the M23, because it is still doing so well. When you've got a car that can win races, why change for the sake of change? Don't change your winning line . . .

Hunt's car was being prepared in the track garages with its new number one painted proudly on the nose in recognition of his champion's status. The year before he had carried number eleven.

The 'off season' had been a short one but there were new cars to be seen in the pit lane: new John Player Special Mk 3s for Mario Andretti and Gunnar Nilsson in the Lotus pit; new smoother shapes for the pair of six-wheeled Elf-Tyrrells, now also carrying sponsorship from First National City Bank Travelers Cheques, and with Ronnie Peterson taking the place of Jody Scheckter alongside Patrick Depailler. Scheckter was in the pit next door, anxiously awaiting his Grand Prix debut with his new Wolf car. John Watson, winner of the Austrian Grand Prix the year before with the Penske team, was now with the Martini-Brabham group following Penske's withdrawal from Formula 1. Vittorio Brambilla was driving for John Surtees instead of March. Clay Regazzoni had replaced Jacky Ickx in the Ensign. The March team were fielding cars for Alex Ribiero, the little Brazilian, and for Ian Scheckter, Jody's elder brother.

The McLaren team plan was to take practice calmly, in order to save men and machines for the race, by running a minimum of laps and then only when there was something to prove. Most teams had run unofficially the day before practice, and although Hunt was against running the car he knew it was an insurance in case the two official practice days were spoiled by rain. Hunt was second fastest to Depailler's Elf-Tyrrell in the opening session of practice, fastest in the afternoon session and faster still the following day, taking pole position.

Five minutes before the end of practice on the first day, a stunning explosion rocked the pits and every soldier within earshot cocked his weapon. McLaren team manager Teddy Mayer dropped between the concrete pit wall and the Armco barrier. 'I knew that if it *was* a bomb there would be bullets spraying everywhere.'

In the instant after the blast, pieces of a black car were raining down at the end of the pit lane, bouncing around on the track, and yet there was no sign of major wreckage. It turned out that the fire extinguisher bottle carrying liquid under high pressure in the nose of Mario Andretti's car had exploded. The force of the blast had blown the nose and front wings off the car and torn back the aluminium chassis of the car as though it was tinfoil. It had ripped off the brake master-cylinders and torn open the front-mounted oil cooler. Without brakes and blinded by oil, Andretti had disappeared down the track, battling for vision and control, which explained the lack of tangible evidence of an accident in the immediate area. Andretti's injuries were limited to oil sprayed back into his eyes and a tingling in his feet from the force of the blast against the pedals.

Weather forecasts in Buenos Aires had predicted rain for the Grand Prix, but it turned out to be a scorching day, and the teams knew that their major problem would be car and driver survival in the heat. Hunt's problems were compounded by the fact that he had forgotten to buy salt tablets before he left Europe, and despite a concentrated search these were unobtainable in Buenos Aires.

The most important thing before a race like this is to make sure your sugar, salt and liquid content is topped up, and I had forgotten my salt tablets. The only thing I could get hold of was medical saline solution, the stuff they feed into your arm through a drip. It was disgusting. I drank one bottle on the Saturday night and one on the Sunday morning. I didn't stop feeling sick until Monday night. I never was sick but I felt as though I was going to be all the time. It really screwed up my stomach.

Several of the drivers had fitted thermos flasks in their cars, filled with a variety of cool drinks. Hunt had orange juice with glucose in it. Peterson had mineral water and glucose. Derek Gardner, designer of the Elf-Tyrrells, said: 'I'm not sure what Patrick's got in his bottle. Some French jollop. Bordeaux I think!'

John Watson was the surprise of practice in Argentina, placing himself alongside Hunt on the front row of the grid in his first race with the 12-cylinder Alfa Romeo-engined Martini-Brabham. When the race started, Watson surged away into a commanding lead. Hunt made another of his poor starts, falling behind Lauda's Ferrari, which he had to re-pass on the first lap, and came past the pits a full three seconds behind Watson. It looked as though Hunt was suffering from his apparent inability to get cleanly off the line, but he says that in this particular race it was part of his scheme.

I wasn't bothered about my start in Argentina. It was rather like a serve in squash. In tennis you try and serve a winner but in squash you serve to put the ball into play. I was only interested in putting myself into play without serving a double fault, ruining the clutch or something. Everyone was a bit marginal on tyres, it was going to be a long, hot race and it would be very easy to be tempted into racing those first ten laps and ruining your tyres. I figured that anyone among the reasonably fast runners who could keep their car, themselves and their tyres in good condition, could drive at eight-tenths all the way and win the race.

For this first race of the season, Teddy Mayer had told both Hunt and Mass that either driver could win if they were able to, but that if they were running in a one-two situation in the lead, the second man was not to try and pass his team-mate.

If I was running anywhere other than leading and Jochen came up behind me, I was to let him through to go ahead and attack. We worked out very definitely that if Jochen could win, he would, unless we were in a leading situation and he had to race me to get past. We didn't have a number one driver arrangement because it was the first race and Jochen was told he could beat me if he was able to, outside the one-two stipulation. This was only fair for Jochen, especially after the second half of last season when all his efforts were concentrated on helping me win the championship.

For five laps Watson held on to his three-second lead over Hunt, with Lauda's Ferrari third and falling back.

The gap to John stayed at +3 each time I passed my signal board but I was comfortable. I was racing at my own speed. There was no hurry. Then suddenly I was catching him at a second a lap and in three laps I was with him. His tyres were going. He'd gone too hard in those early laps. I arrived on his tail as another car came out of the pits and held him up through the Esses. It gave me a run at him and I pulled alongside the Brabham going up to the loop. We were side by side, but I had the line for the corner and after 10 laps I was leading.

As soon as he hit the front Hunt started to pull away. The gap to Watson was 3·5 sec on the 13th lap, 6 sec on the 16th, 8·5 sec on the 19th, 12 sec on the 21st and then he was stroking along in the lead a clear 15 sec ahead of the field. Watson and his team-mate Carlos Pace were nose to tail in second and third places in the Brabhams, with Andretti fourth in the John Player Special. Jochen Mass had been splitting the Brabhams in third place until he spun and abandoned his badly overheated car. The drivers behind him were racing hard but, with a comfortable cushion of time, Hunt was making his own pace with his engine popping and banging on the over run into corners, braking early, taking it easy on his car.

You always drive hard in a race, but you adjust your limits for the car. You look after it, and I was experimenting by slipping into sixth gear down the straight, round the loop and back again, instead of holding fifth, to try and knock the engine temperature back. I had ten degrees in hand on water temperature but I didn't want it to go any higher. Sixth was too high for the loop, it was chugging out of the corner, and I lost a second on my lap time; so I compromised and ran sixth on the straights, dropping to fifth for the loop. I was also braking very early to give the engine more time to breathe. You can

Jody Scheckter

Jody Scheckter probably made a wrong move when he joined the Tyrrell team in 1974, and most people in racing were surprised when he decided to join Walter Wolf's new team for the 1977 season. The South African had matured under Tyrrell's discipline and was convinced that this was the right move; in the opening races this seemed to be confirmed – driving the Wolf WR1 designed by Harvey Postlethwaite he won the opening race in Argentina, he finished second in the South African Grand Prix and led the US Grand Prix West for 77 of its 80 laps before being slowed by a puncture and finishing third.

afford to play with time on braking because it is really only important when you're beside someone, disputing a corner. You can brake 50 yards early for every corner and it hardly shows in lap times.

As half distance came and went it looked as though the season opener would be a cakewalk for the new world champion, who was having an easy race in the baking heat that was playing havoc with drivers and engines. Then on lap 32, as he aimed into the apex of the left-hander in the Esses just after the pits, the McLaren arrowed straight ahead. Hunt fought the wheel and then hit the brakes, out of control as the car ploughed into the catch fences.

You could see the marks on the track. It was 15 or 20 yards before I got on to the brakes and locked them up because I was still trying to get the car to turn.

A bolt had broken in the rear suspension, and as the car went over a hump in the middle of the corner with all the weight on the right rear, the suspension collapsed. Realizing there was no chance of gaining control, Hunt ducked fearing a blow from posts in the catch fencing. The netting fences absorbed the runaway car and although it did hit the guard rails, the only damage was caused by the fencing. The car suffered dented suspension units, torn glassfibre and the damage to the rear suspension that had triggered the accident. It could have been much worse for the team, operating as they were so far from the factory.

Hunt arrived back at the pits on the pillion of a motorcycle, sure that the accident had not been his fault, but not willing to blame a breakage on the car until it had been properly examined. His apparent lack of certainty regarding the cause of the accident immediately afterwards gave pressmen on deadlines the impression that perhaps its could have been driver error, although Hunt was vindicated when the car was brought back to the pits after the race.

The dailies were fair to me but everyone reading between the lines reckoned I'd driven it off the road, thrown away my lead, when it had to be patently obvious that I hadn't. I wasn't prepared to say that something had definitely broken until it had been proved by the team. I'm not prepared to say it as an apparent excuse until I know that something broke. It's unfair to the team. I want them to find out after a proper inspection of the car and for them to say whether it broke or not. This is desperately important for the personal relationship between a driver and team.

While Hunt watched from the pit wall, the race took on a completely new aspect. Watson led again briefly and then Pace went ahead with the Martini-Brabhams close together, first and second and seemingly in command. Jody Scheckter was in third place with the Wolf, having started out in mid-field and driven the car hard for the entire distance. Then it became apparent that the rear of Watson's car was sagging, and on the 41st lap the Brabham literally broke in half when the bellhousing between the engine and transmission gave way. Now Scheckter was second and closing on Pace, who was literally being broiled in a new type of overall he was wearing for the first time. As he was slowed, Scheckter hauled him in and took the lead – in the Wolf pits his wife was in tears of sheer joy. Andretti had passed Pace into second place but with two laps to

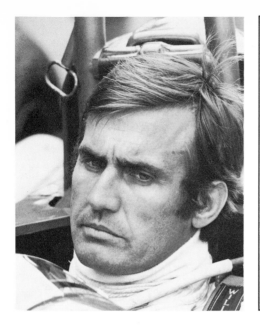

The Hunt mental file card on Carlos Reutemann

Reutemann is as good as anyone else in the world when things are going right – when his car is running well he is unbeatable, and if he gets out in front he will drive absolutely immaculately. He did in several races with Brabham in the BT44 years, and in Brazil in 1977 he was again fast and clean, made no mistakes and drove beautifully.

On the other hand, he cannot salvage bad situations, and his Latin temperament means that when he is down he gets very depressed. He is also easy to 'psych' out, and he doesn't like racing under pressure, especially if it is sustained – he is a very good leader over a short period but he doesn't like being followed too closely for long.

Early in 1977 he had everything going for him. If he gets into a good streak with Ferrari he could win the championship, but if he gets into a bad patch he will have difficulty getting out of it. With Ferrari, it's up to him.

go a rear wheel bearing failed and Andretti stopped. As for Carlos Reutemann, the Argentian driver in the works Ferrari, he had made a pit stop early in the race and had charged back through the field to the wild encouragement of his countrymen.

Support like that from the crowd doesn't make you go any faster because I reckon you're driving as fast as you can anyway, but it gives you a lift to keep you fighting in a situation where you've got to fight.

Scheckter won the race and stepped from his car as fresh as when he had started. Pace crossed the line in second place, his safety harness unbuckled, and climbing up in the cockpit to try and get air. He collapsed when he was helped from the car. Reutemann was third and Fittipaldi fourth. This made three South Americans in the first four, with Andretti classified fifth and Regazzoni sixth to take a point in his first race with the Ensign team. It had turned out to be a freak result, with Scheckter a long-odds winner, but Hunt was delighted for Scheckter's early success with the new team.

I think it's important that a private team should win. It was a lift we needed at Hesketh. When an individual like Alexander Hesketh or Walter Wolf spends all that money and puts in all that enthusiasm, a win like that is an early boost, it encourages the team to keep at it. Obviously it isn't going to be that easy for Jody probably ever again, but it will give the team confidence. They've got that win in the bank, nine points for security and the whole season ahead of them.

I would very much like to have had those nine points myself before the real nitty-gritty racing and the real form starts to show when we get to Europe. Somehow the South American races have always been a warm-up, a good place to get bonus points if you can, but it isn't until we start racing in Europe that the season starts to show a shape and it becomes apparent where team and driver strength lies.

Two weeks later in Brazil James was able to collect six points towards his bonus after finishing second, sandwiched between the Ferraris of Reutemann and Lauda. The race itself had been rather similar to the Argentine GP, with Hunt starting from pole and the McLaren looking the best-balanced car on the São Paulo track. The track has fast straights and writhes back and forth on itself in the infield, with a series of short straights, loops, hairpins and every type of corner to test drivers and engineers. Balance of suspension and brakes, general balance of the overall machine to the circuit was most important . . . and also most difficult to achieve. During practice it became apparent that tyre wear could dictate the race pattern. Then the race organizers had the track washed down over-night before the Grand Prix, and in the morning warm-up the Goodyear engineers discovered to their horror that the cleaned surface had doubled the wear rate.

We were using a soft compound tyre, a quick one, but with a soft compound you've really got to give it some thought. Will it last the distance? In fact we allowed for too much understeer on my car, the front tyres wore out and my pit stop to change them was the difference between winning and losing. Reutemann was 11 seconds ahead at the finish and he said he had only enough rubber left for two more laps. Then he would have had to stop for a change.

Carlos Reutemann
chasing Hunt in the
1977 Brazilian
Grand Prix. The
Argentinian went
on to win the race.
After a pit stop Hunt
finished second

There is more to racing than merely driving faster than the next man. As in backgammon you have to play several moves ahead, log the tactics of your opponent in your mind, and play at speed. Hunt plays backgammon with his long, thick fingers whisking the board in sleight-of-hand movements, playing fast, thinking hard, adjusting his game to the throw of the dice. In the car his mind works the same way.

In the Brazilian Grand Prix he was aware of a tyre problem, aggravated by the washing-down of the track, but he was still playing moves that would keep him in the lead and counter the second placeman at the same time – playing a winning and a blocking game at the same time. For once Hunt made what he felt to be a reasonably good start from pole position, but the sensation was local hero Carlos Pace, who stormed through from the third row of the grid and charged into the lead.

I couldn't beat the starter of the race, Pace.* He went and the starter pressed the button for the green light. But we expected him to come through. He could call the tune from back there but on the front row we had to wait for the light. It wasn't too bad down into the first corner with Pace a bit excited rushing down there with Reuters as well in the Ferrari but it's South America and you know that's fair enough, you bear it in mind and not get involved.

Hunt went past Reutemann on the third lap and then started to push in on the leader, but although he could bring the nose of the McLaren to within five yards of the Brabham's gearbox – the ideal distance for a 'tow' in the slipstream – the Brabham simply pulled

---

* In some races in Latin countries, it has become almost traditional for local hero drivers to be given the benefit of any doubt in dubious starts . . .

away on the straight. At the end of the long downhill straight there is a fast, banked right-hander like an Indianapolis curve. It was here that Pace made the mistake that cost him his lead, perhaps the race. He went wide of the racing line into the shaly gravel where the track had been starting to break up during practice, and spun sideways. Hunt dived for the gap and snatched the lead.

He must have got his car half sideways and then it hit because I felt something touch as I went through. It must have been his nose against my back wheel.

Six laps were gone in the Brazilian Grand Prix and the man the crowd of 80,000 had shouted for, chanting themselves into a frenzy of excitement before the start, was limping to the finish with the nose of his car tearing itself away and a damaged radiator. It had all the makings of a repeat of Argentina, with Hunt pacing himself at the start, biding his time and then making his move. He was in the lead now, with a gap opened to four seconds over Reutemann, but already he knew his front tyres were wearing too fast because there was too much understeer, too much 'ploughing ahead' in corners for the good of the tyres. Yet it had been important for him to be in the lead, clear of the other cars.

If you're in the turbulence behind another car you don't have front end grip and your car is sliding more than it should. On your own you can call the tune.

Jochen Mass in the other McLaren was on Reutemann's heels, with the black Lotus of Mario Andretti in behind him. 'I was taking bets with myself every lap round that he'd lose it next time through,' drawled Andretti. 'I tellya. You know how slippery it was getting at the end of the straight, and I was nibbling in. I knew I couldn't pass him there because I didn't have enough, but I was nibbling and he thought I would try and pass and he started going in harder and HARDER and wider and WIDER until WOW!' Mass skated into the catch fencing, throwing it back into the path of Regazzoni's Ensign, which became hopelessly entangled. Depailler spun the six-wheeler Elf-Tyrrell, and team-mate Peterson, storming down into the long surve, saw the carnage ahead, tried to brake hard, skated wide of the line and spun backwards into the fence. Depailler scrambled back on to the track only to crash again later in the race at the same point, ploughing into Mass's already wrecked car.

Andretti had been ready for Mass to over-reach himself and he slipped through unscathed to chase Hunt and Reutemann. Now the power play started. Hunt was endeavouring to ease back his lead to conserve his front tyres as much as he dared, while at the same time trying to suck Reutemann into his slipstream and tempt him to wear the Ferrari's tyres faster. Andretti, tucked in behind Reutemann, was working on the same plan. 'My car was runnin' just a little smoother than the other two through the turns and I knew if I could keep the pressure on Reutemann I KNEW I could get rid of him. I was lookin' good, I tellya . . .' But the Andretti optimism was to be defeated by an electrical failure a few laps later and he was out of the race. Jody Scheckter, winner in Argentina two weeks before, was already out with a seized engine in the Wolf.

By half distance Hunt was really in serious trouble with his tyres and simply playing for time, gambling that he could regain time lost in a stop for new tyres with increased speed.

I had been hoping that Reutemann was having the same trouble so I was really holding him back, but when he came past me he just rocketed away. That's when I knew I had to stop and change. You don't like throwing away the lead on a tyre change if there's a chance that everyone else has the same trouble. I reckoned I could go three seconds a lap faster on new front tyres and there were twenty laps left. It would be worth the pit stop. It was also saving me from the chance of a front-end blow out with a tyre wearing right through. If you have a front-end failure you go straight on into whatever you're going to hit, but if you have a rear blow out you tend to spin and scrub off speed.

My pit thought I was signalling for rear tyres but as I came down the pit lane and saw the rears ready I pointed to the fronts, so it didn't really affect the race outcome too much. Maybe lost me a few seconds. That's one of the situations where if we'd had radio communication with the pits I could have told them of the problem and they would have been ready.

The pit stop took perhaps fourteen seconds, and Hunt came back into the race on Lauda's tail in fifth place. In a lap he had passed Lauda and Watson's Martini-Brabham and was third but a long way now behind Reutemann and Tom Pryce, the Welshman in the Shadow, who had worked his way into second place, helped by the crashes and the rash of pitstops around him. But six laps later Pryce's car was stopped at the side of the track and Watson was also out. The order remained the same to the finish, with Reutemann sending the crowd into a delirium at the front, Hunt somewhat less popular in second place, and Lauda third, having fought through from a seemingly impossible grid position.

The Driver

I think I can improve, although I am not sure that I can drive much faster than I did in 1976, when at times I was driving as fast as I possibly could, which is not necessarily the same as driving as fast as it is possible to drive. I can see areas where I can improve.

I want to see if there is an ultimate limit at which one can drive, and drive to that all the time, or at least as close to it as I possibly can. Then I want to couple that limit with a similar level of aggression. In 1976 I had a couple of brushes with other people because I was driving absolutely on the limit and going for every opportunity, and now I want to drive at that level without having the brushes. Some drivers, Niki and Emerson for example, have successfully kept away from brushes as they have matured, and you must be able to do that. But I have noticed, more with Emerson than Niki, that they have achieved that by backing off just a little. Overall, their driving has probably improved, and they have got better results that way. I want to get even better results, without brushes and without ever backing off at all. Only experience can give me that.

It is not in Hunt's nature to rest on his racing laurels, and in modern racing a driver has to be able to do much more than race. He has to have obvious abilities in terms of skill and speed, but it has more and more become important for him to be something of an expert in setting up a car – knowing its behaviour under an infinite variety of circumstances, knowing how to cope with and cure not only the blatant symptoms of oversteer and understeer, but the more complicated issues of balancing a car aerodynamically, suspension adjustments, and tantalizing changes between different compounds of tyre and the changing behaviour of the tyres themselves during a race. All these factors become a science in themselves. Being brave isn't enough any more, when the entire grid of 25 or so cars can be covered by less than two seconds difference between the pole man and the slowest car in the field.

I know what I want out of my car. I know when it's right and when it's wrong. When it's wrong I play with it . . . we don't always go in the right direction but that's a problem of combination between me and the team. At least when we head in the right direction I can always tell them quickly. I'm not a very technical sorter. A lot of drivers think they've got to go madly technical on a car, but I'm a positive believer in keeping everything simple. We know that that's how you should build racing cars, we know that the simpler it is, the better it is – that's an indisputable fact of motor racing – and we know that organizing everything simply is better. So why not keep sorting – setting up – simple; think as simply as possible. There are a lot of drivers who think that the more they say, the more they'll impress everyone. There are some drivers

Preparation. In clothing, as in cars, every precaution is taken to protect a driver from fire – here Hunt adjusts his fire-resistant underwear and balaclava.
As he is strapped tightly into his M23 (lower) the pipe of the life-support system can be seen leading into his helmet

who can move a roll-bar* a quarter-of-an-inch and come in with a story that will last 15 minutes about all the differences it's made to the car. Well that's all absolute rubbish . . . all it does is confuse the team.

If they make a change to the car and it makes no difference it's much better to say it makes no difference than to create a difference. That's how people can be sent up blind alleys of development. It's essential to do something only if it's positive. That way you can sort it out quickly. Jochen Mass has had trouble sorting his car in 1976 and while it's exactly the same as mine, he tends to go off on complicated side tracks and get into a mess with his car from time to time. Apart from the three races in the middle of the 1976 season when we had that drama with the oil coolers under the wing, I never had a problem . . . we always managed to get the car right. I'm convinced that half the battle is to keep it simple and the other half is to know what you want. . .

In practice before the final race of 1976 I couldn't get the car right and I was coming in and out of the pits all the time, which is what you've got to do because it's not a lot of use soldiering on around the track if the car is obviously wrong. At the end of the day we took a long hard look at the car, took an objective view of ourselves and the other teams, and it became apparent that the people who had been playing with their cars and trying to sort them out – Ferrari and McLaren – had done a lot worse than the people who had just got out there and stuck to it. We decided that it was the sort of track you just couldn't get the car 'sorted' for. It was understeering in the slow corners and oversteering in the quick ones. We made a positive decision then that in the final timed session on Saturday, we wouldn't play with the car. We would put it back to standard, go out very quickly to balance it – change the wing angles, the roll bars and fit new tyres – then I would go out and drive it hard. That's what we did and I ended up on the front row of the grid beside Andretti. You've got to be positive in spotting these things, and then getting on with it.

Teddy Mayer says Hunt's strong point as a test driver is that he is intelligent and able to learn to drive around a problem, to recognize what the problem is, without necessarily being terribly technical. 'We didn't really do that much development on the M23 in 1976, but he certainly knows when a car is unbalanced and has a reasonable idea of what is causing it – or which end of the car, at least. That might sound a bit strange because you would think it an easy thing to know, but it isn't. Very often a driver will say the car oversteers too much when this oversteer is actually induced by understeer initially and he hasn't recognized this. James normally does.'

Discussing Hunt's progress as a team driver during his first season with McLaren, Mayer found it difficult to pinpoint any serious shortcomings. It was an arrangement that had worked out more successfully than they had dared to hope when the contracts were signed in December 1975. 'I think he's a much more mature person now than he was at the start of the year. Possibly his initial shortcomings were that he didn't like taking decisions. He had been in a team where all the decisions were taken for him, where "Bubbles"

*The link between suspension units side to side, controlling the degree of roll during cornering.

Horsley told him exactly what to do all the time. At McLaren Racing we think that it's better for a driver to learn to take his own decisions because he has more information available to him and this is where a more mature driver will ultimately do better. As team manager I want to be able to contribute to the choice of tyre or choice of settings on the car, but ultimately the driver has got to say, and I think initially James wanted us to do that . . .'

Earlier in 1976, Hunt had compared the Hesketh and McLaren management approaches for Pete Lyons in an *Autosport* interview.

With Hesketh we used to spend a lot of time examining ourselves. 'Bubbles' used to exercise tremendous discipline. I would actually get into trouble with 'Bubbles' if I talked to anybody else after a practice before I'd sat down and he'd wrung the truth from me and we'd all had a big post mortem.

McLaren don't give me any discipline at all. They let me do exactly what I want to do, they don't take any notice of me. The debriefing sessions we have at McLaren aren't the same sort of thing at all. We discuss something if we feel like it, but if nobody wants to talk we don't.

The lack of a firm directive from his pit in the closing laps of the 1976 Japanese Grand Prix had infuriated Hunt when he looked for positive instructions on what to do about his tyres. Mayer agrees that the position was a difficult one. 'It was a situation where almost any decision could be wrong or probably *would* be wrong. James would have liked us to make the decision for him. On the other hand almost every team manager I've spoken to feels as I do, that he had more information than we had. In addition, if we had brought him in 30 laps from the end when tyres were beginning to be a problem – running the "wets" with the track now dry – there was the possibility of brand new "wets" destroying themselves even quicker than the old ones were doing, because that had happened with several cars. So you can't say the decision was wrong or right . . . I don't feel it's defensible or indefensible . . . it was there and it worked out. And he won the World Championship.'

Everything is subordinated to the car, and driving it, and Hunt tends to adopt a 'corner is a corner is a corner' approach to circuits. Such as they are, his preferences have little to do with a track as such, but with its environs, the hotel the team uses – better still if several teams stay in the same hotel and there is a party atmosphere.

Race tracks seem to be like tennis courts, the place you do your business. You play tennis on a different surface from time to time or you go to a different type of track. But the real business is driving the car. Obviously some tracks are safer than others, and one is keener to race on the safe ones.

I never had to make a conscious effort to have preferences, and it happened that I never did. Years ago I struggled on street circuits to an extent, because I didn't realize that a different technique was required and I used to bounce off kerbs too much and damage wheels. But that was before I got into Formula 1.

Physical fitness is almost taken for granted, perhaps because it is something Hunt has never had to work at, and he dismisses the training sessions which some teams outside Grand Prix racing have set up almost with contempt.

A racing driver has got to be in good condition physically, but he is not an

Olympic athlete and doesn't have to be trained like one. If you can't get fit enough to drive a Grand Prix car just by leading a perfectly normal life you don't deserve to be racing a car. I find my training – maybe half an hour a day – is a good discipline for me, and I do it as much for my mental discipline as for my physical condition. When you are into something like this you have to apply a sort of total concentration. You need to be fit enough, and after that it is all down to your mental approach – that really is the important thing.

Something of the stress a racing driver can work under comes through as Hunt turns to diet, to storing the energy his body will burn up during a race:

Usually I try to eat plenty of solid food the night before a race, and I have breakfast on the morning of a race. When you are nervous it is a lot easier to go without breakfast, so to eat a normal breakfast on race morning is something of an effort. I have eggs, usually scrambled because they are easy to digest, and toast because bread has plenty of starch and that's good for stamina. Marathon runners and other endurance event men train on starch, bread and potatoes, a week before a race, but as I don't much like either bread or potatoes I've got a problem.

His concentration when he is away from the circuits is on the future, although not the immediate future of tactics for the next race, and on the Grands Prix. He points out that, increasingly, different sets of skills are required for each category of racing.

We have got to the point now where each formula is specialized. For example, I know that I could not walk back into Formula 3 and consistently win races – I would have to get the feel of it, and learn it again. I can go to the States for a Camaro race and put a car on pole, as I did in 1976, or put it on the front row as I did in 1975. But as soon as the flag was dropped in those races I was completely at sea because it is a very different sort of specialist racing.

However, with the world championship under his belt, his thoughts did turn to driving in the very different world of American track racing:

I would be prepared to have a go at the Indianapolis 500, even though it would be a big gamble. I am confident that I could do the job, as far as sitting in the car and driving it fast is concerned, but the race is a whole different game in terms of tactics, and knowing how to handle it in the racecraft sense is where I would be at a big disadvantage against the USAC drivers.

But along with many other things that is secondary. Formula 1 comes first – and proving that as world champion he has to be rated more than a good Grand Prix driver; his strongly competitive nature means that an over-riding motivation is rubbing in as a fact that he is 'the best'.

I intend to keep going full chat until the day I retire, because it makes sense. Life's too short – it certainly can be in a racing driver's career – to relax. You don't stand any less chance of getting killed if you relax – an accident which starts at 165 mph is as bad as one that starts at 170 mph.

The danger aspect is the biggest cloud on my horizon, and a constant heavy thought at home – it's not something to think about in the emotionally charged atmosphere at a circuit. One has to weigh the odds, the risks involved, as well as one can and look at life and see if it is worth taking the risk for the time being. Once you have decided it is, then it would be counter-productive to worry about it. In fact, worrying about it would be very bad for your driving.

Once an accident has started happening, you've just about got time to say 'shit, I'm having a shunt'. You can't usually do anything about the fact that you are having an accident, but you might have time to get the car to go in backwards rather than forwards, which hopefully would be better. Basically you have just got time to get your head down and brace yourself . . .

You might as well give it your best while you are racing, and then stop at the right time.

Four Formula 1 Seasons
James Hunt's Record

1973

Race of Champions, Brands Hatch*	Surtees TS9B	3rd
Monaco Grand Prix	March 731	9th
French Grand Prix	March 731	6th
British Grand Prix	March 731	4th
Dutch Grand Prix	March 731	3rd
Austrian Grand Prix	March 731	ret
Canadian Grand Prix	March 731	7th
US Grand Prix	March 731	2nd

1974

Argentine Grand Prix	March 731	ret
Brazilian Grand Prix	March 731	9th
Grande Premio Presidente Medici*	March 731	ret
Race of Champions*	Hesketh 308	ret
South African Grand Prix	Hesketh 308	ret
Silverstone International Trophy*	Hesketh 308	1st
Spanish Grand Prix	Hesketh 308	10th
Belgian Grand Prix	Hesketh 308	ret
Monaco Grand Prix	Hesketh 308	ret
Swedish Grand Prix	Hesketh 308	3rd
Dutch Grand Prix	Hesketh 308	ret
French Grand Prix	Hesketh 308	ret
British Grand Prix	Hesketh 308	ret
German Grand Prix	Hesketh 308	ret
Austrian Grand Prix	Hesketh 308	3rd
Italian Grand Prix	Hesketh 308	ret
Canadian Grand Prix	Hesketh 308	4th
US Grand Prix	Hesketh 308	3rd

1975

Argentine Grand Prix	Hesketh 308	2nd
Brazilian Grand Prix	Hesketh 308	6th
South African Grand Prix	Hesketh 308	ret
Silverstone International Trophy*	Hesketh 308	ret
Spanish Grand Prix	Hesketh 308	ret
Monaco Grand Prix	Hesketh 308	ret
Belgian Grand Prix	Hesketh 308	ret
Swedish Grand Prix	Hesketh 308	ret
Dutch Grand Prix	Hesketh 308	1st
French Grand Prix	Hesketh 308	2nd
British Grand Prix	Hesketh 308	4th
Swiss Grand Prix*	Hesketh 308C	8th
German Grand Prix	Hesketh 308	ret
Austrian Grand Prix	Hesketh 308C	2nd
Italian Grand Prix	Hesketh 308C	5th
US Grand Prix	Hesketh 308C	4th

1976

Brazilian Grand Prix	McLaren M23	ret
South African Grand Prix	McLaren M23	2nd
Race of Champions*	McLaren M23	1st
US Grand Prix (West)	McLaren M23	ret
Graham Hill International Trophy*	McLaren M23	1st
Spanish Grand Prix	McLaren M23	1st
Belgian Grand Prix	McLaren M23	ret
Monaco Grand Prix	McLaren M23	ret
Swedish Grand Prix	McLaren M23	5th
French Grand Prix	McLaren M23	1st
British Grand Prix	McLaren M23	disq
German Grand Prix	McLaren M23	1st
Austrian Grand Prix	McLaren M23	4th
Dutch Grand Prix	McLaren M23	1st
Italian Grand Prix	McLaren M23	ret
Canadian Grand Prix	McLaren M23	1st
US Grand Prix	McLaren M23	1st
Japanese Grand Prix	McLaren M23	3rd

* Non-championship races.

Index

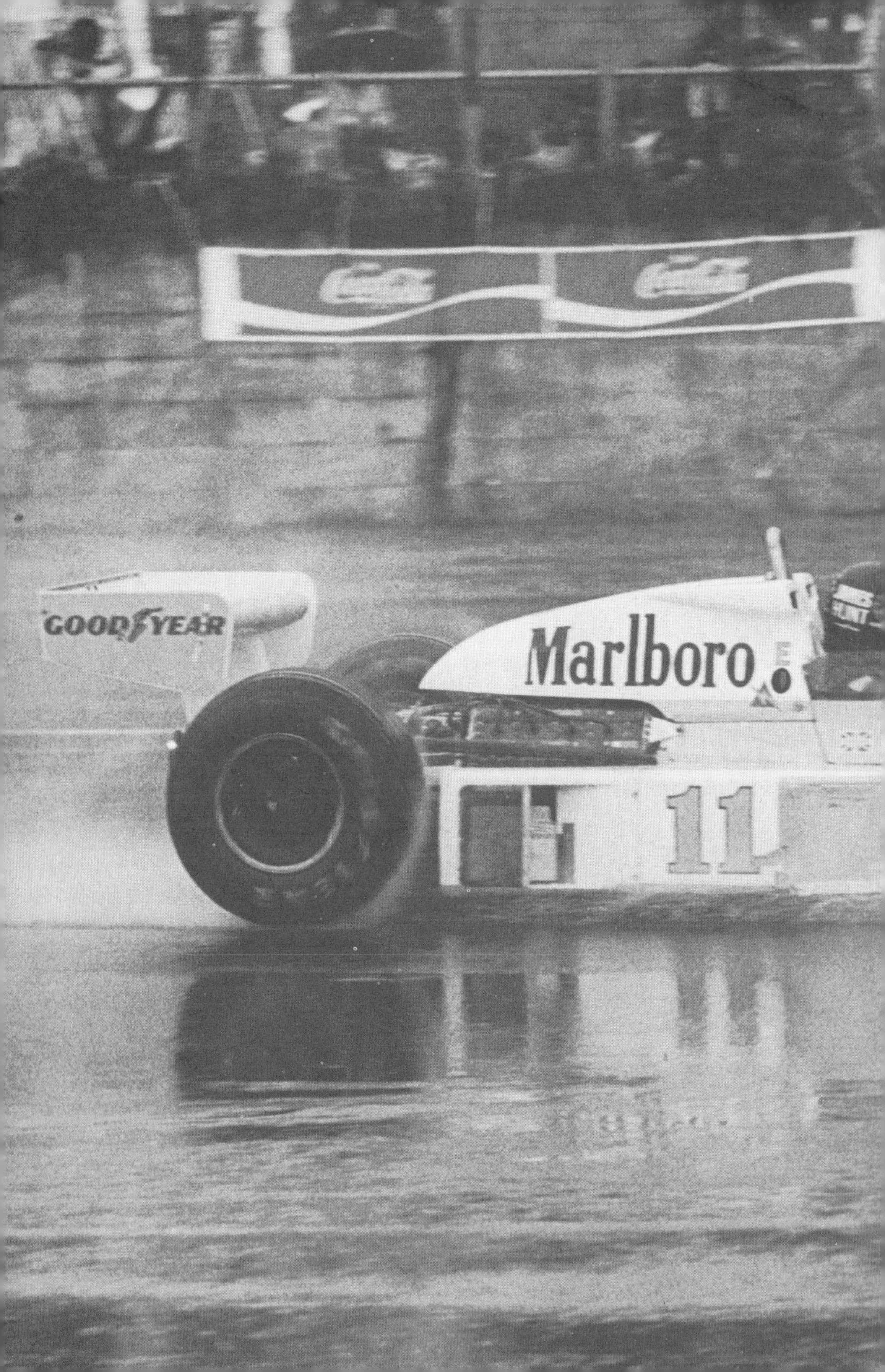

GOODYEAR
Marlboro
11